THE ART OF THE DIORAMA

BY RAY ANDERSON
PHOTOS BY ROLAND PATTERSON

Editor: Bob Hayden
Art Director: Lawrence Luser
Assistant Editor: Marcia Stern
Cover photo by Chris Becker

The material in this book first appeared as articles in FINESCALE MODELER Magazine

First printing, 1988. Second printing, 1989, Third printing, 1994.

The art of the diorama

Part 1: Choosing a subject for
a scene that tells a story

BY RAY ANDERSON

PHOTOS BY ROLAND PATTERSON

Author Ray Anderson, shown here with a wild assortment of his favorite 60 mm scale diorama characters, has built over 100 boxed dioramas. The scene shown here has a much larger "footprint" than the compact scenes he recommends.

THIS ARTICLE is the first in a series devoted to designing and building boxed dioramas. Over the past 15 years I've built more than 100 such dioramas, and I hope to pass along many of my ideas and techniques to *Fine-Scale Modeler* readers.

No other kind of modeling grabs and holds viewers like a diorama, because a diorama tells a story. In fact, the roots of the word "diorama" mean "a story in the round." Many of us have childhood memories of marveling at life-size dioramas in natural history museums, and miniature boxed dioramas are just as popular. I've watched museum visitors take time to examine all the details in miniature dioramas, while other seemingly more spectacular exhibits rated only a passing glance. Why?

Why dioramas are popular. A boxed diorama is a complete package that combines sculpture, painting, fine craftsmanship, and even custom lighting in a self-contained unit. However, the reasons for its popularity are far more complex than simple appreciation of the skills required to execute the work. At its best, a diorama is not a simple static model, but an art medium capable of conveying a tale, a mood, or even evoking an emotional response. Because of this complexity, choosing the subject matter and designing the diorama require attention to artistic principles that most modelers may not be familiar with.

William Wilson, an art critic for the *Los Angeles Times*, explained the popularity of miniatures with two words: "realism" and "intimacy." The two characteristics are related, because only by employing realism can the diorama involve the viewer in the scene. Once the viewer, even briefly, accepts the scene as the real world and not just a model, we can achieve intimacy. In the next article I'll discuss how even a small scene can be designed to surround the viewer, to give the impression that he is part of the scene.

Choosing a scale. The scale of the models in a diorama is an important consideration. One critical factor is the "footprint" of the scene — that is, how much horizontal space it occupies. After building many dioramas I'm convinced that the scene should be as compact as possible, and that the footprint should be small. While I've made several scenes with 75 mm figures (roughly 1/24 scale), the majority have been 60 mm (about 1/30 scale).

The 75 mm size is appropriate when there are six figures or less. A small footprint is still possible with this number of figures, although it takes more time to create the figures in this scale, and because they are larger they are prone to damage in handling.

The 60 mm size is better when there

Fig. 1. "A Problem on the Powder River" is a subject with plently of dramatic action. Such scenes quickly involve the viewer; Ray reports that upon seeing the precarious position of the figures in a similar diorama, one visitor asked half-seriously, "What right do you have to play god and endanger those men?"

are a large number of figures or the scene will contain massive structures. I find it easier to convert Historex 54 mm figures to this scale than to scratch-build larger figures, and a variety of horses and other accessories are available. Although it is a greater challenge to add fine detail in this scale, the smaller, lightweight figures can be placed in more precarious poses with less chance of handling damage. Finally, the compact footprint possible with the 60 mm size makes scenes as small as 4" x 6" feasible.

Choosing a suitable subject. Because a boxed diorama is a major

project, considerable thought should be given to selecting the subject. Let's look at subjects from a variety of perspectives.

From the standpoint of constructing the scene, the easiest subject matter is a building interior, which requires only woodworking skills. Next in complexity comes a building exterior, where some sky background and earth or paved foreground are required. Then come rock formations with sky backgrounds, and finally the most complex scenes, where the foreground extends all the way back to the horizon without interruption.

Another way to consider subject matter is by the degree of activity to be shown. Action scenes are among my favorites, and I find figures in extreme poses ideal — their flying clothing and hair, extended fingers, and other details add much to the three-dimensional effect of the work, Fig. 1. And, because action can forcefully portray the critical moment in a story, action scenes are good at putting a story across to the viewer.

Scenes depicting historical events, Fig. 2, are common subjects, but after building a great many of them I've come to the conclusion that such scenes can be boring. Few viewers are interested that every campaign ribbon and decoration is present on a tunic, or that the beadwork on a war shirt is accurate, and the historical significance of the scene isn't always obvious. I've decided that historical subjects should be spiced up with one of the techniques discussed below.

Pieces that have personal significance for the builder or owner are both emotional and popular. A personal diorama can portray the old family farm, Fig. 3, or a memorable family incident; "Ettie Belden's $15 Russell," Fig. 4, is a good example. The Favell Museum of Western Art acquired a rare painting by famous cowboy artist Charles Russell, and I was asked to build a diorama showing the history of the piece. I spent many pleasant hours with the Beldings' granddaughter gathering background information, then, based on ranch furnishings that still exist and family photo albums, the scene evolved.

More than half of my dioramas portray the American West, so I should touch on this as subject matter. Much

has been written about the popularity of all forms of art that deal with the old West, which was, in fact, a brief moment of history peopled by characters in drab clothing. In spite of that, twentieth-century Americans see it as a period in our history when people were industrious, adventuresome, and enjoyed life. Dioramas showing this period simply take advantage of this popularity.

Showing the passage of time. In some dioramas time is the subject. By placing two scenes with identical perspective and subject matter in the same outer case, they can accurately portray the passage of time.

I built such a box to portray the Anasazi, the early cliff dwellers of the American Southwest. The first scene shows the Indians ascending onto the plaza through a small opening in the

Fig. 2. (Left) This historical scene shows John of Gaunt (father of King Henry IV of England) in 1359. The significance of subjects from history isn't often apparent to the viewer, and the author has decided that such scenes need to be "spiced up."

top of their underground kiva, or ceremonial lodge. It is a night scene with pale blue light; they are preparing for a dance. A bright orange light emanates from the kiva roof opening.

The second scene is about 600 years later. The kiva roof has collapsed, and the identical stone structures on the plaza show the ravages of time and weather. A park ranger is explaining the kiva to a group of overweight, camera-laden tourists in Hawaiian shirts. Warm sunlight in the second scene contrasts with the eerie lighting in the first.

Subjects with a purpose. Dioramas can also be created for commercial purposes, and in such instances the purpose will have a lot to do with the subject matter. An ornate building or a two-story outhouse from a Western ghost town would be an interesting addition to an architect's office. A humorous scene of the old West with a circuit judge holding court in a saloon — the

dispute is over the sale of an old horse, which is *in* the saloon, of course — would be a good conversation piece for a lawyer's office.

A diorama could be the prize for a church raffle, perhaps with the stained glass window that will be bought with the proceeds shown in a renaissance setting; an opera or stage-play diorama could be used in a fund-raising campaign for a performing arts group; a snake-oil salesman working a crowd in a small town would make an ideal award for a sales competition.

Fantasy scenes are in a category all their own. Although the figures, background, and lighting offer unusual creative opportunities limited only by one's imagination, Fig. 5, there's a drawback to fantasy subjects: One goal of a good diorama is to involve the viewer in the scene, making him a part of it. Except for kids, who bring their vivid imaginations, involving the viewer may be a problem with fantasy pieces,

Fig. 3. (Below) "The Morrison Place" was an attempt at a still life — a scene without figures. Instead of people the viewer must relate to the numerous details, such as the tombstones under the tree. The discarded Campbell Soup can to the right of the gate adds both a spot of bright color and a familiar object that every viewer recognizes.

Fig. 4. "Ettie Belden's $15 Russell" depicts a true incident. Etta Belding is shown receiving the painting, which was a wedding anniversary gift from her husband. Charlie Russell, their cowhand, was present. The painting hung on the parlor wall for decades; it's now in a museum.

simply because, by definition, they present situations most viewers can't relate to.

So what makes a good diorama subject? In 1972 I created what I thought was another routine diorama, but to my surprise it received international recognition. I realized that there must be some ingredients accidentally included in the scene that made it so successful. Some 8 years and 35 dioramas later, I had identified most of the elements, and I've incorporated them in many subsequent scenes. Here they are:

● A diorama should tell a simple story, the conclusion of which may be left to the viewer's imagination. You can hold the viewer's attention for a minute or two at most, so the clues to your story must be simple and obvious. (I've found that it's difficult to contrive fictional incidents that are as interesting as the real thing. I read of an old prospector who spent his whole life looking for gold only to die without finding any, but while digging his grave his friends struck it rich. Figure 6 shows my version.)

● The piece should be as small as possible to create a personal, intimate feeling. The figures should be "small jewels," not "statues."

● The scene should surround the viewer, making him feel part of the action instead of remote from it. (A playwright I know made an interesting observation about dioramas. In regular stage plays the "fourth wall is up" — the actors interact with each other, but they ignore the audience, which views the scene from a distance. But in musical comedies they "lower the fourth wall," and the players speak to and interact with the audience. In dioramas we want to lower the fourth wall to involve the viewer.)

● Ornate building interiors are generally more effective than outdoor settings.

● There should be many minute, eye-catching details. I call these "Camp-

Fig. 5. "The Swamp" is one of the author's few fantasy dioramas. While fantasy subjects are fun for the builder, involving the viewer in the scene can be difficult because both the setting and the characters are intentionally unfamiliar.

bell Soup Cans"; Fig. 3 shows why.

● Lighting should be indirect, often coming from the side to provide high shadow relief.

● Most scenes can be effective without dramatic action. When dramatic action is involved, it should never include violence — let the murders, assassinations, and beheadings take place offstage, in the viewer's imagination.

● Elaborate costumes are great attention getters and crowd pleasers. This makes scenes from the twelfth to the eighteenth century highly suitable subjects.

● A proper balance of construction time is approximately 50 percent for the scene and background and 20 to 30 percent each for the figures and the outer case.

● The overall effect of the diorama and outer case should be that they were created during the period depicted, Fig. 7.

Like any long list of rules, these ten factors aren't meant to apply all at the same time to the same diorama. Instead, understanding the reasoning behind each is the key to coming up with interesting scenes.

The role of humor. You'll note that humor isn't listed as a separate element; this is because an attempt should be made to include it in most scenes. While many viewers are turned off by serious or unpleasant subjects, humor has universal appeal. Humor also helps break down the "fourth wall" by providing the viewer with something he can easily relate to.

I recently completed a series of boxed scenes depicting the internment of Japanese-American citizens during World War Two. This was one of our country's least-noble episodes, and the scenes easily could have been done as a protest, but instead the people who had been interned wanted the scenes to incorporate all the details of camp life. There was humor in the scenes — one boy is shown protesting to his mother about having to run the gauntlet of his friends to empty the chamber pot in the latrine at the far end of the barracks row — and this humor holds the viewer long enough to put across the inhumanity of the larger circumstance.

The outer case: an integral part. It's also important to consider the outer case design while selecting the subject. The outer case is an integral part of the overall concept and should reinforce the subject matter.

The ideal location for a scene is on a bookshelf at eye level, where it can be observed either from a distance or up close. Scenes may be flush-mounted at eye level in a wall, or freestanding consoles can be used to display them.

Finally, always remember that the purpose of the scene is to tell a story. Although the viewer may marvel at

Fig 6. "The day Jeb finally hit paydirt" is based on a true story. Let your eye travel around the scene and take in the details: the bonnet hung on a tombstone, the prospector's mule loaded down with gear (and eating the funeral wreath!), and the fellow at lower right filling his boots with gold nuggets.

the intricacy and skill used to create the work, in the end the success of the diorama depends on arranging the models in such a way that they create a memorable aura, mood, or idea.

That's more than enough theory. Diorama construction involves a number of skills, including mechanical design, woodworking, plastics, sculpting, painting, and some electrical knowledge. In the next installment of this series we'll start on these how-to aspects with an article covering diorama layout and design. **FSM**

Fig. 7. "By courage I repel adversity" is a historical scene that portrays Robert de Mamines, Knight of the Golden Fleece. Note how the finish of the outer case supports and adds to the impact of the diorama inside it.

The author's "Il Gigante" portrays the sculpting of Michelangelo's colossal "David" in 60 mm scale. The scene is compact despite the huge subject (the real "David" is 14 feet tall!): the diorama fits in a box only 1 foot wide and deep.

The art of the diorama

Part 2: Designing boxed scenes

Figs. 3 and 4. Where you place the horizon has a lot to do with the subject of the scene. In "Muckwa's Mountain" (above) the horizon is low because the location is a high pass; "Chichen Itza" (below) employs a high horizon to emphasize the depth of the Mayan sacrificial well.

BY RAY ANDERSON

**PHOTOS BY
ROLAND PATTERSON**

BOXED DIORAMAS have to be planned. When you're painting on canvas or sculpting in clay it's relatively easy to correct mistakes, but altering a boxed diorama is difficult, particularly when details that establish the composition have been nailed down. Because of this, taking adequate time to plan a diorama project is a necessity, not a luxury, and extra care in design will save construction time.

Making preliminary sketches. Having said that, I have to admit that I find it difficult to make useful preliminary front-view sketches of boxed scenes. Such sketches seem to hamper the spontaneity of the scene. Instead, I make a simple plan view — I call it a "footprint" for the diorama — and a side elevation drawing of the box. In

producing these working drawings I establish the overall size of the box, and ensure that the figures, background, and details will fit. (Although the drawings are reproduced smaller than actual size for the magazine, it's important that you plan full size right from the beginning.)

Often your choice of subject matter will dictate how you go about designing the scene. If there are several figures, they should be sculpted before the scene is laid out; when structures will dominate the box, they can be roughed out first.

Using perspective. To be manageable boxed dioramas must be compact, but how can we convince the viewer that mountains are 20 miles away or a canyon is a mile deep when the space we have to work with is less than a foot? One trick we can use is perspective, Fig. 1. In this typical outdoor scene the horizon is near the center of the scene and all perspective lines con-

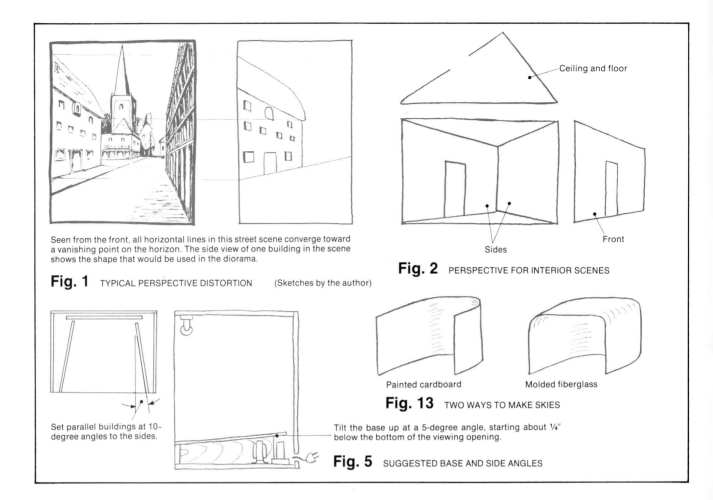

Seen from the front, all horizontal lines in this street scene converge toward a vanishing point on the horizon. The side view of one building in the scene shows the shape that would be used in the diorama.

Fig. 1 TYPICAL PERSPECTIVE DISTORTION   (Sketches by the author)

Fig. 2 PERSPECTIVE FOR INTERIOR SCENES

Ceiling and floor

Sides

Front

Painted cardboard   Molded fiberglass

Fig. 13 TWO WAYS TO MAKE SKIES

Set parallel buildings at 10-degree angles to the sides.

Tilt the base up at a 5-degree angle, starting about ¼" below the bottom of the viewing opening.

Fig. 5 SUGGESTED BASE AND SIDE ANGLES

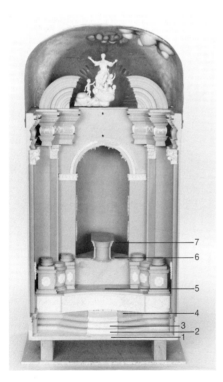

Fig. 6. Ray decided perspective was inappropriate for the interior of his Benedictine Abbey. Instead, he used a succession of terraces (numbered here) to suggest that the scene was receding from the viewer and enhance the illusion of depth.

verge at a vanishing point on the horizon.

The side view of a building wall from the same scene shows how all horizontal surfaces slope toward the vanishing point. Note how the windows at the rear of the scene are narrowed and foreshortened, and that there are few right angles. Figure 2 shows how this is applied to a building interior; note how the floor and ceiling slope, and that the corner of the room is an angle greater than 90 degrees.

If you want to delve into perspective theory, any library will have several books that cover the subject. For the purposes of diorama building, however, we'll use a few simple procedures to avoid getting all tangled up in our underwear while laying out the converging lines.

The first step is to determine where the horizon will be. It is usually at the midpoint of the front opening, but there will be exceptions. If the viewer is riding down a street on horseback the horizon will be lower than if he were walking. To emphasize the feeling of height, Fig. 3, the horizon should be low, but a few subjects require that the horizon be near the top of the box, Fig. 4.

After locating the horizon, we establish the angles of all surfaces that radiate from the horizon and vanishing point. Make the bottom of the scene (the ground or floor) slope up at an angle of 5 degrees, starting from ¼" to ⁵⁄₁₆" below the bottom edge of the front opening, Fig. 5. When rows of buildings are parallel, angling them in about 10 degrees provides realistic perspective. The roof slopes of tall buildings require severe perspective distortion.

To evaluate — and adjust — the angles, mock up the building walls using thin cardboard cutouts. It often takes several tries to find the right angles, and you can plan on wasting a lot of cardboard, but not a lot of effort!

In designing outdoor scenes without buildings you need only be concerned with the horizon, the 5-degree ground slope, and the ¼" step from the ground to the bottom edge of the viewing window. The rest of the scene can be eyeballed. If a stream runs through the scene, plan to incline its surface at the 5-degree angle, but tilt the stream bottom more severely, so the stream becomes deeper as it nears the front of the box.

Laying out interior scenes. For interior scenes, 95-degree corners usually appear realistic. Often, strict rules of perspective must be tempered by practical considerations. Door and window heights will be determined by the figures adjacent to them, and vice versa: The figures in the rear of the scene may be only 50 mm to 54 mm tall compared with their full-size 60 mm compatriots up front.

Once the heights of the windows and doors have been established, the foreground wall height can be determined by trial and error (and again, lots of cardboard). Be sure to cut out all windows and doors in the mockups.

It often takes several sets of cutouts to come up with a scene that combines pleasing perspective, a practical box size, and a workable front opening. With the mockups and a cardboard front frame in place eyeball the scene from the intended viewing position. The final design is always a compromise: Often you'll have to change the shape of the front opening or alter the depth of the scene.

Incidentally, I find that it requires less brain power to use the metric system in laying out my scenes. For example, if you need 40 floorboards running from front to back in a cabin, it's easier to calculate the width of each as it narrows toward the rear of the scene if you use metric measurements.

Occasionally I've built a scene where I found it impractical to use perspective. My Benedictine Abbey, Fig. 6 (shown in color on pages 47 and 48), was a such a subject; in it I had to resort to achieving a perspective-like illusion by posing the scene on several steps, or terraces. In this scene and many others I also use the simple trick of placing numerous obstacles along the eye path to the rear of the box to enhance the feeling of depth.

Staging the action. The next step toward your final design is to firm up the figures. I make a list of the figures with a brief description of body position, assigning a letter to each. Next, on an 8½" x 11" sheet of paper I sketch a rough footprint of the scene, with small lettered circles to represent the figures and numerous notes to myself on the background treatment, Fig. 7.

Gradually the scene fleshes itself out. The list of figures becomes more and more detailed as physical characteristics and costume notes are jotted down for each. You are, in fact, casting the scene as if it were a movie or play, and you need to think long and hard about how each player in the scene relates to every other actor — if someone has no specific function, "fire" that fellow!

Next, start building the figures. Establish their poses and overall shapes, but don't complete fine details such as fingers yet, because the figures will be handled a lot. Tape your rough footprint to a slab of cardboard included at 5 degrees, and temporarily position the figures by poking their mounting wires

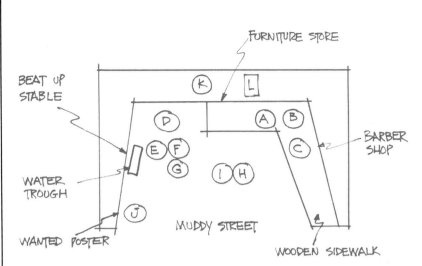

Fig. 7 THE SCRIPT AND STAGE DIAGRAM

A. SHERIFF WITH LEFT ARM IN BLOOD STAINED SLING, HAT, STAR BADGE, POINTING TO Ⓛ WITH RIFLE IN RIGHT HAND, HANDLE BAR MOUSTACHE.

B. CUSTOMER IN APRON, BALD, FACE LATHERED

C. REAR VIEW OF BARBER, SHAVING MUG IN LEFT HAND, RAZOR IN RIGHT HAND.

D. TALL, GAUNT MINISTER IN BLACK SUIT, MUTTON CHOPS, MUDDY BOOTS, POINTING WITH LEFT HAND TO Ⓛ HOLDING UP BIBLE WITH RIGHT HAND, MOUTH OPEN, FACING VIEWER, STANDING ON DRY SPOT.

E. WOMEN HOLDING UP SKIRTS, STANDING IN MUD,

through the paper and into the cardboard, Fig. 8.

Now view the scene through a cardboard mockup of the front opening and adjust the positions of the figures. To keep the footprint small, move the figures as close to one another as possible. Remember, we want to surround the viewer and involve him in the scene, so one of the ways we can save space is to bring the action right up to the front glass.

Many first-time diorama builders make the scene too large, and especially too deep. Most boxed dioramas should be less than 10" deep, and 12" is the maximum depth you should ever consider. In fact, rarely does any dimension, width, height, or depth, of my boxed dioramas exceed a foot by more than an inch or two, Fig. 9.

Next, temporarily mount the cardboard mockups for walls or buildings that you made earlier, and add a cardboard background with the horizon line. Hold up your cardboard viewing opening and take a hard look at the

mockup, Fig. 10. You may find that, with the figures in place, slight corrections in the perspective lines may be required. Make adjustments, then examine the scene again to see where it can be condensed — I always try to save even ⅛".

Dimensions for the outer box. We are now ready to complete the design. To draw the final top view, start with the front opening as the base line and locate the structures on a clean sheet of paper, taking dimensions from the cardboard mockups.

Next, locate the blocks that will be used to mount the walls or structures to the base, Fig. 11. The structures will be a minimum of ¼" thick and the blocks another ¾", and once you've drawn them the width of the scene — the inner assembly in our boxed diorama — is established.

If you've held the depth of the scene to a minimum, the box should not have to be much more than 10" deep. With the inner assembly flush with the front of the outer box, allow ⅜" to ½" clear-

Figs. 8 and 9. (Below) An important step in planning any diorama scene is to work with the figures on a rough cardboard base. Here the temporary base has been inclined at the 5-degree angle to be used in the final box. (Above) A view of the scene before painting shows how the figures have been brought up to the front edge, and how little depth is required even when the action requires lots of figures.

Fig. 10. The same scene, with a cardboard front frame held in place to evaluate the perspective and placement of the figures. Ray suggests doing this with cardboard building mockups instead of the nearly complete buildings shown here.

Meet Roland Patterson

Roland Patterson got started in photography in the 1940s, working part time at the Wichita *Beacon*. During World War Two he took photographs in the Army, and afterward attended the Art Center School in Los Angeles.

After part-time work at a *Life* magazine lab as an assistant photographer, he returned to the Midwest under contract to Black Star Agency, which handled photo assignments from most national magazines. More than a decade later he moved back to the West Coast and went into advertising photography.

When, more than a dozen years ago, he took over photo chores for several model magazines, Roland met diorama builder Ray Anderson. He was impressed, he told FSM, that Ray's modeling "always began, not with a manufactured kit, but with an idea," and he's been shooting remarkable photos of Ray's work ever since. (His self-portrait shows him photographing angels dancing on the head of a pin.)

ance at the rear (something unforeseen always seems to happen back there) and about ¼″ clearance on each side, and draw the outline of the outer box. For your first scenes, you may want to play it safe by allowing extra clearance between the inner assembly and the outer case.

Now, with the width of the outer box and the location of the viewing opening known, you can calculate how wide the front frame should be. Typically this dimension is 2½″, but it may vary from 2″ to 3″. Make sure the frame is wide enough to cover the raw front edges of the inner structures.

Next make the final side-view drawing, Fig. 12, which includes the outline of the outer box. Approximately ¼″ below the front opening, draw the ground level or floor, sloping up at 5 degrees. Rough in the structures, but don't worry about their details. The primary purpose of this view is to position the lighting components.

Lighting considerations. Although lighting will be covered in a separate article, during design we must allow

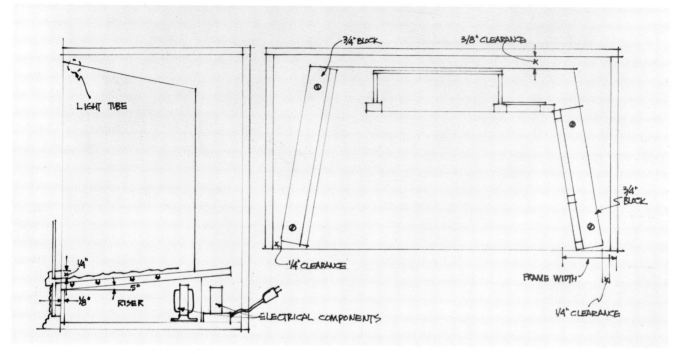

Figs. 11 and 12. Final construction drawings for a typical boxed diorama, shown here approximately one-third actual size. Note the locations of the risers, the blocks to hold the walls, and the placement of the lighting components.

sufficient space for the lighting components. About ⅛″ in from the front edge, add a vertical line from the underside of the ground surface to the inside of the outer case. This is the front edge of a ¾″-thick riser that runs from front to back in the box.

The rear edge of the riser will be determined after the ballast and starter are spotted. Standard fluorescent ballasts are 1¼″ x 1¾″ x 3″; "banana" ballasts are 1″ x 1″ x 5¼″. The starter is 1¾″ high. Remember that the inner assembly is inserted and removed from the front and the electrical components should not interfere with doing so.

When the ballast and starter positions have been determined, we can turn to the lights. In most scenes the light will be attached to the top front of the outer case, mounted as close to the front edge as possible so the viewer can't see it. (For a few indirect lighting applications, the light may have to be attached to the inner assembly.)

Each light requires its own starter and ballast, and two 110-volt lines run from the light to the ballast/starter. Make sure you provide clearance for the wires, particularly for the lights mounted at the top front. I usually mount a pushbutton on/off switch on the left side, at the lower rear corner.

Making a sky. The sky can be handled in two ways. The simplest is to use a curved piece of cardboard, Fig. 13, on the three sides, and paint the inside top of the outer case the sky color. The joint between the cardboard and the case top is not distracting, and this method is best for your first boxed diorama.

Fig. 14. The completed scene shown in the previous photos. It depicts a noble procession at Augsburg, Swabia, in 1501, and appears in color on pages 28 and 29.

A more ambitious approach to the sky is to make a male mold and lay up a four-sided fiberglass shell with curves that join the sides, back, and top. I'll discuss this technique in a future article.

Until next time. In the next installment I'll start discussing how to translate your paper drawings and cardboard mockups into the final boxed scene, Fig. 14. While researching and building the figures and details, you'll start "living" in the scene. You'll begin to see how the rocks will fall, where the blacksmith keeps his tools, where clothing will be tattered and stained, and

how a spittoon has splattered the wall. As the little details fall into place your scene will become realistic and "lived in."

More about that next time. In the meantime, grab a few sheets of paper and some scrap cardboard and start planning your first diorama! **FSM**

The surveyors in "Piety Hill" are the key to the story: A new county road is to be built through the property and all the history wrapped up in the old church and its graveyard will be lost. The figures in this scene are 60 mm tall, roughly 1/30 scale.

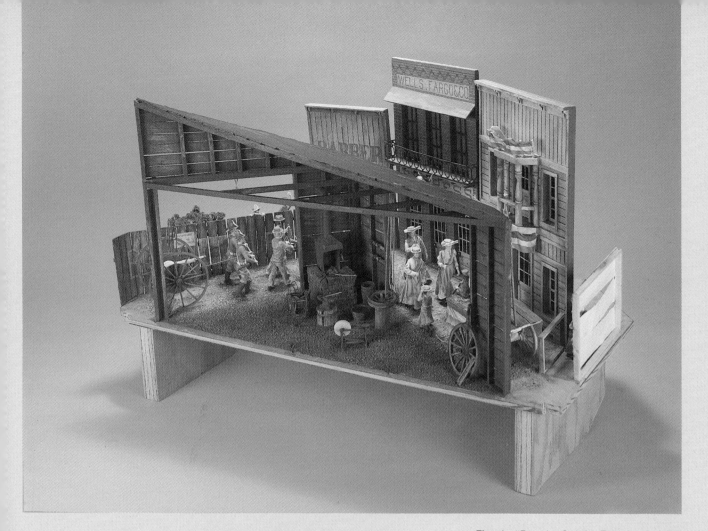

The art of the diorama

Part 3: Techniques for building boxed scenes

Fig. 1. "Perry's Creek, Fourth of July" shows how a typical diorama inner scene is built. The unusual viewpoint for this diorama is from inside a darkened blacksmith shop; the main action — the Independence Day parade — takes place outdoors in the bright sunlight.

BY RAY ANDERSON

PHOTOS BY ROLAND PATTERSON

W HILE THERE'S NO RIGHT or wrong way to build a boxed diorama, over the years I've managed to come up with a system that I like (and that works). In this installment I'll illustrate a couple of ways to tackle the task. My approach will be to outline the general construction steps that are common to all the boxes I've built, presenting detailed information on a few specific scenes along the way.

As explained in the last installment, each of my boxed dioramas consists of an outer box and a separate, stage-like scene which slides into the box, Fig. 1. We'll cover construction of the outer boxes in a future article; this time we'll take a look at how to build the inner scenes.

Framing "standard" scenes. The

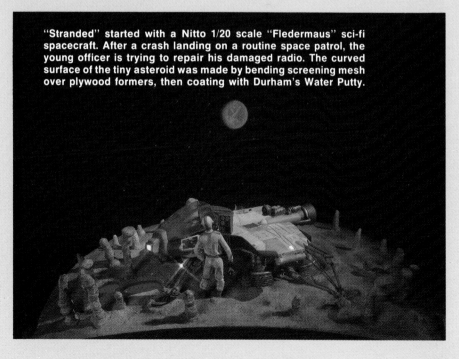

"Stranded" started with a Nitto 1/20 scale "Fledermaus" sci-fi spacecraft. After a crash landing on a routine space patrol, the young officer is trying to repair his damaged radio. The curved surface of the tiny asteroid was made by bending screening mesh over plywood formers, then coating with Durham's Water Putty.

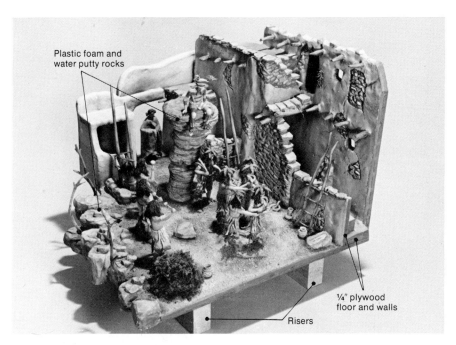

Plastic foam and
water putty rocks

¼" plywood
floor and walls

Risers

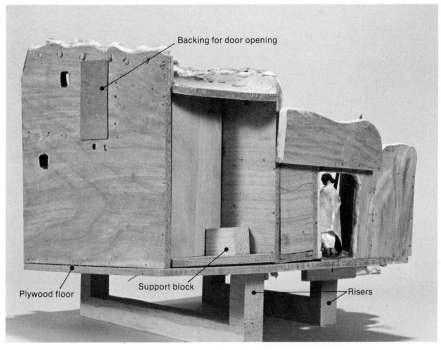

Backing for door opening

Plywood floor

Support block

Risers

Figs. 2 and 3. Front and back views of "Snake Dance, Walpi," an outdoor scene with masonry walls on two sides. Although the diorama includes materials as diverse as epoxy putty, plastic foam, wood, and styrene, except for the figures most of what you see is textured and painted Durham's Water Putty. All photos on this spread by A. L. Schmidt.

plywood may be overlaid with wood or other material, sealed and painted to represent paint or wallpaper, or covered with Durham's Water Putty to simulate rock or masonry (see page 22). Where water putty is to be used I prefer model airplane plywood for its superior resistance to warping.

Free-standing buildings, such as the church on page 14, are also built from wood. Here again I start with a ¼" plywood form, cut window and door openings, and build up details with sheetwood and stripwood. The techniques I use are commonplace for wood models, so I won't elaborate on them here.

Rugged terrain. Building irregular landscape, Fig. 6, is more involved. Because the figures must be rigidly bolted to the plywood underframe, the first step is to make the figures and mount them on stout wires (we'll cover figure construction in the next installment). Then I position the unpainted figures on wood blocks of the appropriate heights to establish their three-dimensional relationships with one another.

After noting the dimensions (back and up) from the front edge of the scene to the mounting wire for each figure, I use the measurements to develop a footprint, or plan, of the rock formation. This is used to make irregular plywood formers (the shapes are often complex) and to locate them where the figures can be securely bolted to them, Fig. 7. Occasionally I have to drill some of the mounting holes before the inner frame is nailed together and covered with non-rusting screen.

Once the shape of the scenery is established, I make rock faces from plastic foam coated with Durham's Water Putty. The foam is cut to form the basic rock formation, working around the mounting wires for the figures. After the main rock formation is coated with water putty, carved, and detailed I add individual rocks, then paint.

Rock faces aren't the only kind of terrain where the screen mesh and water putty technique is required. When I set out to model a tiny, 116'-diameter asteroid in "Stranded" (page 15), the best way to achieve a convincing surface curvature was to start with screening. The odd, stalagmite-like rock formations were made on plastic foam cores.

A note about trees. When a diorama scene requires trees, Fig. 6, I make them from scratch — not from bits and pieces of natural growth. I feel strongly about this: Because trees must fit into the diorama rock formations and figures, I think it's a waste of time to try and find the ideal real branch that will complement the composition. Worse yet, when you find a detailed piece of natural growth there's a temptation to compromise the design to use it. That's a compromise we can't afford if we are

basic materials for most scenes are ¼" plywood and 1" pine. I use the pine to make risers that bring the floor of the scene up to the bottom of the viewing opening, Figs. 2 and 3. The risers are tapered — short at the front, taller at the back — to tilt the floor of the scene at a 5-degree angle as it recedes from the viewing opening. I sometimes deliberately leave the inner box risers a little short so I can add shims to bring the scene up to the correct level without exposing the front edge.

The plywood floor is screwed and

glued to the risers. This construction provides a rugged base and furnishes a rock-solid mounting surface for figures, furniture, and details. In ornate interior scenes I frequently make the floor a separate piece. This facilitates painting the walls and also makes it a good deal easier to tackle such things as painting complex rug patterns.

Where walls are needed, as for an interior scene or an outdoor setting that includes buildings, I also start with shapes cut from ¼" plywood, Figs. 4 and 5. Depending upon the subject, the

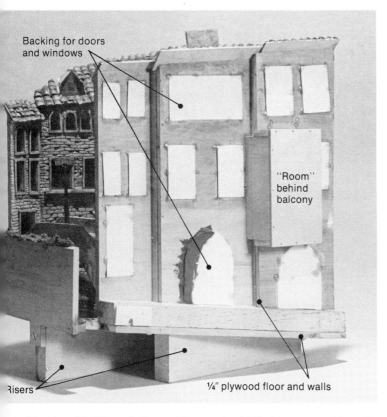

Backing for doors and windows

"Room" behind balcony

Risers

¼" plywood floor and walls

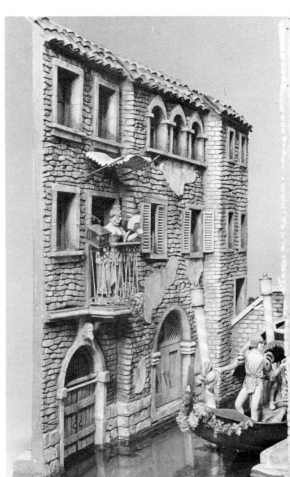

Figs. 4 and 5. "Venezia," a canal scene in old Venice, removed from its outer box. Although both the subject matter and the overall shape are radically different, note the similarities in materials and construction to the "Snake Dance" scene on the opposite page. (See page 20 for a color photo of this diorama.)

to do the best possible job of putting the story of our diorama across to the viewer.

The photos tell the rest of the story; I hope you won't be dismayed to learn that what I've said so far is everything I have to say about building the inner scenes of boxed dioramas. We'll cover the boxes themselves in a future installment, and I plan to talk about lighting in a separate article. The use of plastics, particularly to simulate water, will also rate a separate installment — but until then, try a scene without water!

Next: building and painting figures. After building over a hundred boxed dioramas, I've reached the conclusion that figures are the heart and soul of every scene (and, incidentally, that diorama stories without figures don't work particularly well). In the next installment I'll review techniques for converting diorama figures from Historex 54 mm figure parts, then explain my painting methods. **FSM**

Figs. 6 and 7. "Muckwa's Mountain" is the story of Indians who meet a bear (Muckwa) unexpectedly. The rock faces and irregu-

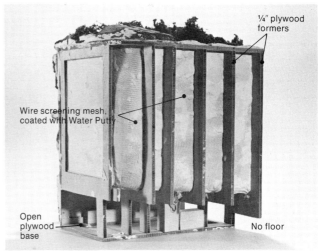

¼" plywood formers

Wire screening mesh, coated with Water Putty

Open plywood base

No floor

lar contour of this scene required that it be constructed using plywood formers and mesh screening as described in the text.

The Secret of Diablo Canyon shows the type of rock and coloring typical of the American Southwest. The groundwork, rock formations, and individual rocks are all made from Durham's Water Putty.

Fig. 3. The earthen huts in *When They Made House Calls* have the same kind of screening base used for making irregular terrain forms. Note the realistic, gritty dirt texture achieved by applying dry Water Putty powder over a wet base.

Fig. 9. Ray's *Hopi Snake Dance* shows the crisp stone detail that can be reproduced with Durham's, and how a second coat of putty can be added over some areas to represent adobe.

Making realistic diorama groundwork, rocks, and masonry

Versatile techniques from a master diorama builder

BY RAY ANDERSON

PHOTOS BY ROLAND PATTERSON

OVER THE YEARS I've developed my own set of techniques for diorama groundwork and stone modeling based on a single easy-to-find and easy-to-use material: Durham's Water Putty. With just a little practice, a few simple tools, and one or two other common materials you can duplicate any groundwork texture or rock formation. Follow along and I'll show you how.

Durham's Water Putty, Fig. 1, comes in a white, yellow, and red cardboard container and is available in most hardware stores. It is a fine, off-white powder that is mixed with water to make a plasterlike material with consistencies ranging from heavy cream to stiff clay. Durham's dries hard, is strong, and does not shrink, but its main advantage over plaster is its sculpting life, during which it sets, but remains leather-hard and workable for about an hour. Its natural color is a pale tan, but it can be colored with powdered cement or grout colors, as well as painted.

Making basic groundwork. The diorama base material I usually use is ¼" plywood. I drill ⅛" holes on 2" centers partway through to firmly lock the groundwork in place. For uneven terrain I substitute non-rusting screen (aluminum or fiberglass), Figs. 2 and 3. I glue figures or vehicles to the base with ¹⁄₁₆" pads under them so the groundwork material can flow under and around the models for a clean, realistic appearance, Fig 4.

Before pouring the basic groundwork, glue rocks or other details that will be embedded in the ground in place. Make mud puddles as shown in Fig. 4. Nail thin strips of wood faced with masking tape to the edges of the base. These strips serve as temporary dams to hold back the poured water putty.

Incidentally, pouring groundwork for the first time on a completed diorama scene with painted figures and vehicles is a traumatic experience, so it's a good

idea to practice. Make 2" squares of ¼" plywood for test samples, drilling locking holes as described above. Nail wood strips around the edges and test different colors to see how you like them and learn how the Durham's sets and works.

Whether it's the real thing or practice, the plywood subbase must be level, because the Water Putty mixture has to be fluid enough to flow. Moisten the plywood before pouring the putty mixture over it.

Mix a batch of Water Putty to the consistency of thick pancake batter. It's easy to mix Durham's too thick — after all, the label says "putty" — but if you do the material won't flow readily and may set up before you can finish texturing it. Moistening the plywood helps overcome this, but the real answer is to keep the putty mixture thin — almost watery. If you decide to color the groundwork with cement color, moisten a small sample to check the color first, and bear in mind that only a little color is needed.

Once mixed, it's important to pour the wet groundwork quickly, and all at one time. Fill a couple of paper drinking cups with Durham's powder so you can whip up additional batches quickly if needed. Pour the mixture onto the moistened plywood — a ¹⁄₁₆"-thick layer is sufficient — and spread it around with an old brush or bent wire. Wet the brush frequently with water while pushing and leveling the mixture, and use a V-shaped cardboard trough to run putty into the back corners of the scene. If some of the poured putty gets onto a figure, wait until it dries to remove it.

Dry texturing. The next step is to add dry Durham's powder over the wet poured coat. The water from the poured coat soaks into the dry powder, moistening it and bonding it in place, so the wetter the poured coat, the deeper the final texturing. The poured surface should have a moist sheen; if not, brush on more water.

Fig. 7. The canyon walls and free-standing rocks in *The Stalkers* are plastic foam coated with Durham's. Ray's techniques for simulating water with plastic compounds are explained starting on page 50.

Fig. 10. The masonry buildings, bridge, and stonework at the edges of the canal in this boxed scene, *Venezia*, were all made from Durham's Water Putty.

I sprinkle the colored powder onto the wet base using a large vitamin bottle with a ¼" copper tube about 4" long attached to the cap, Fig. 1. Tapping on the bottom of the bottle makes the powder flow, and you can direct it wherever it's needed. Use plenty of powder and don't worry about getting it on the figures, but try to keep the figures dry so the powder will not adhere to them.

Coat the entire surface of the groundwork with dry Durham's powder, working around the corners until all moist spots are covered up. Don't disturb the models in the scene, and even if the di-

orama is a real mess at this point — it will be — don't panic.

For groundwork about ¹⁄₁₆" thick leave the diorama undisturbed for 24 hours. Then turn the scene upside down over a trash can and gently tap the bottom to dislodge the surplus powder. Use a small brush to remove more loose Durham's, then, in a well-ventilated area (preferably outdoors) use the air blast from your airbrush hose and a small bristle brush to dislodge the rest of the loose particles. Scrubbing vigorously with an acid brush with the bristles trimmed to about ¼" long results

in a realistically gritty dirt texture.

Clean up areas around the figures' feet and embedded details with a dental tool, and press footprints and wagon ruts into the dry powder using wood tools dipped in water.

Dirt isn't the only ground texture you can make with Durham's. The smooth, featureless surface of snow can be made by eliminating the dry powder step of the technique — just pour the wet mixture and allow it to dry. I make cracked mud flats the same way, omitting the dry powder treatment and adding cracks with a dental chisel when the putty becomes leather hard.

I color groundwork with Humbrol or other flat enamel paints, and the colors I choose depend on the locale and type of terrain I'm modeling. Keep in mind that the colors lighten considerably after the solvent evaporates, and that it often takes several tries to get the proper shadows. Start by painting in the dark shadow colors, placing the deepest shadows under the figures or other freestanding objects. Once you are happy with the shadow colors, dry-

Fig. 5. The puddle in the center of *The Coming of the Killer Whale People* is styrene, installed before pouring the ground-work. Most of Ray's boxed dioramas are based on Historex 54 mm figures converted to 60 mm — roughly 1/25 scale.

brush the groundwork with two or more highlight colors. Finally, add a shiny glaze to areas that are supposed to be damp or wet, Fig. 5.

Making rocks and boulders. I form individual rocks by adding a ¹⁄₁₆″ shell of Durham's over a plastic foam core. The best plastic foam to use is the porous, open-cell kind obtained from craft shops, not the shiny-skinned type used for packing materials. Rough out the rocks and boulders with an X-acto knife, making a batch of a dozen or more at once to save time. Skewer each chunk of foam on a toothpick, Fig. 6, which will serve as a handle until the rock has been painted.

Mix a batch of Durham's to the consistency of cream and dip each chunk of foam into it. Pull the rock out of the liquid and twirl the toothpick between your fingers (doing this in a paper cup helps keep the liquid from going everywhere) to fling off the surplus putty. Fill larger holes where the putty has

Fig. 8. *Paiutes 3000 B.C.* depicts the interior of a cave that overlooks a valley — and an unwelcome visitor in the form of a small wooly mammoth! Note the sharp horizontal cuts in the rock, and the blackening caused by soot from cooking fires.

Fig. 1. Materials and tools for diorama groundwork and rock making. (Clockwise from center) Durham's Water Putty, dry powder dispenser made from a plastic vitamin jar and ¼″ I.D. copper tubing, plastic foam and toothpicks for rocks, palette knife, dental tools, and acid brushes, and tongue depressors and cups for mixing the putty.

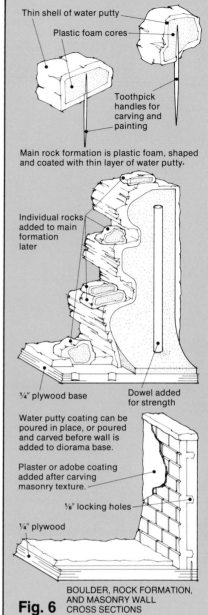

Thin shell of water putty

Plastic foam cores

Toothpick handles for carving and painting

Main rock formation is plastic foam, shaped and coated with thin layer of water putty.

Individual rocks added to main formation later

¼″ plywood base

Dowel added for strength

Water putty coating can be poured in place, or poured and carved before wall is added to diorama base.

Plaster or adobe coating added after carving masonry texture.

⅛″ locking holes

¼″ plywood

Fig. 6 BOULDER, ROCK FORMATION, AND MASONRY WALL CROSS SECTIONS

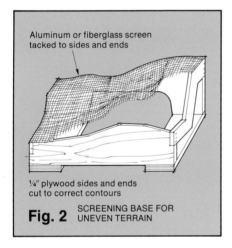

Aluminum or fiberglass screen tacked to sides and ends

¼″ plywood sides and ends cut to correct contours

Fig. 2 SCREENING BASE FOR UNEVEN TERRAIN

not taken hold with an old brush, but remember that this is only the base coat and a perfect shell is not critical.

Stick the toothpick into another block of plastic foam and let the rock dry for at least a few hours.

Next, dip the rock into a thicker putty mixture, the consistency of heavy cream. This is the final coat. Remove excess putty and drips with a palette knife, and as the putty begins to set, start shaping the rock with the palette knife.

Don't try to refine the detail too much at first — the idea is simply to form the basic shapes during the early drying stage of the putty. As the putty reaches its leather-hard stage, use your modeling knife to carve in strata, de-laminations, and other textures. As the putty continues to harden, I use a dental chisel to add cracks and veins. It takes me about four passes at each rock to finish it.

Eroded sandstone will tend to be cylindrical and have a heavy horizontal texture. This can be done by making horizontal cuts with the dental chisels and blending with an old brush and water.

Painting individual rocks. I usually finish the rocks before gluing them to the groundwork. The painting technique depends upon the type of rock. Darker, more dense rocks are first painted with a light color such as Humbrol Unbleached Wool (MC30) or Unbleached Linen (MC25). These are light grays and tans. When dry, the rocks are painted with a wet wash of Humbrol Olive Drab (HM3). Most of the color is then removed with paint thinner, so that only the cracks and other textured surfaces retain the dark color, Fig. 7. Several applications of washes may be necessary. The highlights may be cleaned off with Kleenex moistened with paint thinner, and some streaks of green or a warm tan such as Humbrol Desert Yellow (93) added.

Southwestern rocks should be warm colors, such as yellows, oranges, and browns. In addition to darker, colder colors, I give dense, granite-type rocks a coat or two of Grumbacher matte varnish, which adds a nice sheen to them.

Modeling large rock formations. To make the large rock formations in my boxed diorama scenes I start by gluing large chunks of plastic foam (I use

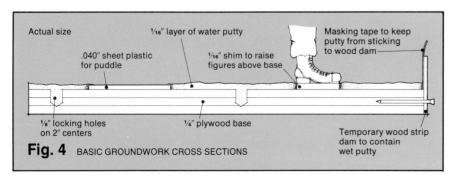

Actual size

.040″ sheet plastic for puddle

1⁄16″ layer of water putty

1⁄16″ shim to raise figures above base

Masking tape to keep putty from sticking to wood dam

⅛″ locking holes on 2″ centers

¼″ plywood base

Temporary wood strip dam to contain wet putty

Fig. 4 BASIC GROUNDWORK CROSS SECTIONS

The irregular terrain of *A Paiute Predicament in High Rock Canyon* consists of Durham's Water Putty applied over a screening base supported by a simple plywood framework.

white glue) to the plywood base. Since some structures may be 12″ high and only 1½″ deep, I dowel the foam pieces in place as well, for strength, Fig. 6. Shape the foam with carving knives, modeling knives, and coarse foam files. Just do the basic rock structure, as the individual rocks will be added later.

Before you start building, spend some time thinking through your rock formation. Where would faults occur? Where would smaller pieces have fallen? Where would erosion have taken place? Taking the time to think it through will add to the realism of the finished piece.

After the foam rock formation is roughed out brush on a coat of Durham's. When it dries, go back and remove the loose particles, deepen the cracks, and add details. For the final coat, limit your working area to about 4″ square. Apply a thick, heavy coat, and as it begins to set, start working in the details. The tendency is to start this phase too soon, so try to wait.

You'll have to go over the surface four or five times, adding more detail with each pass. If you break through the skin, add more putty, and keep in mind that loose particles are easier to remove as the putty dries. Work your way around the rock formation a 4″ square at a time. The exact textures depend upon the type of rock formation

you are modeling — the soft sandstones in many of my western scenes are textured with sharp horizontal cuts, Fig. 8, then blended with an old brush and water or finished smooth with a finger. For my work, I find *Arizona Highways* magazine an excellent reference for rock formations.

When the basic rock formation is finished, add the loose rocks. Moisten each spot with water and use thick Durham's as the bonding agent. Think through the scene and visualize where the rocks would have fallen. How has erosion affected the rock formation? There may be room for gravel washes in the larger gaps between boulders.

Painting techniques for rock formations are similar to those for individual rocks, but require more thought. Ask yourself questions as you go along: Should there be pockets of moss under the ledges? Would these surfaces have been discolored by water runoff? Do you want to add pools of water and glossy water seeping from the rocks? Take your time and enjoy the questions (and, as you come up with them, their answers); this is the fun part of diorama modeling!

Modeling masonry walls. I usually start building walls by cutting their shapes from ¼″ plywood and drilling locking holes to help the Durham's get a good grip on the wood, Fig. 6. If I add

the walls to the scene before working in the surface texture, I position the scene so the plywood is horizontal and use masking tape or wood strips to contain the putty.

Spread a coat of thick, tinted putty ¹⁄₁₆″ to ³⁄₃₂″ thick on the plywood. When the putty sets to the point that it can be cut without tearing, cut in the stone or brick pattern with a narrow dental chisel. Next, start shaping individual stones — don't try to add too much detail on this first pass, just outline each stone. Then rework the wall area by area, a 4″ square at a time, alternately deepening the gaps between the stones and shaping the stones themselves, Fig. 9. It takes four or five passes to bring out all the detail. Remember that the harder the putty, the cleaner it will cut.

I've also built up brick walls, Fig. 10, using individual pieces cut from cast putty sheets. Line a shallow box with plastic food wrap, pour in the putty, and let it dry thoroughly before you saw out individual bricks. The sheet of putty will be brittle; cutting it requires care.

And that just scratches the surface! I'm sure that once you've used Durham's Water Putty to make groundwork, rocks, and masonry you'll develop other modeling uses for it. I hope to read about them in the future. **FSM**

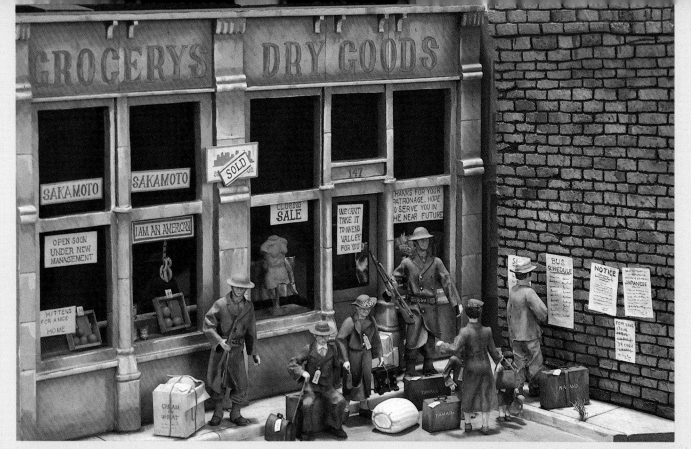

Fig. 1. This is one of three scenes from a display titled "Internment at Manzanar," which tells the story of Japanese-Americans confined during World War Two. Note how all surfaces in the scene, with the exception of the storefront glass, have a dead-flat finish.

The art of the diorama

Part 4: Figure conversion and painting techniques

BY RAY ANDERSON

PHOTOS BY ROLAND PATTERSON

A DIORAMA is a scene that tells a story, and nothing helps tell a story quite as well as human figures.

Virtually all my figures (at last count over a thousand of them) are based on lightweight 54 mm scale plastic soldiers from Historex. This French company makes a large line of styrene Napoleonic soldiers, and it's easy to convert them into all sorts of subjects from prehistory to today. The plastic is hard, white, and takes fine detail, and the figures come as separate body parts. My techniques are explained in detail in the comprehensive article that begins on pages 28 and 29, so I won't repeat them here. Instead, we'll concentrate on painting.

Paint and painting tools. For realism, I use flat paints for everything in the diorama that is not supposed to be shiny or wet, Fig. 1. I use Humbrol

modeling paints because they yield a dead-flat finish, have a finely ground pigment which doesn't obscure delicate detail, and above all, dry rapidly. I use the same paint for all the details in a box to achieve consistency; in fact, where I've use real cloth or cord in a box I've found the best strategy is to use flat varnish to kill the shine, then paint and shade the material with Humbrol, just as if it were plastic.

My painting tools are simple. I use a ferris-wheel arrangement, Fig. 2, to store the paints and a baking tin to hold miscellaneous tools and six shot glasses. Three of these contain lacquer thinner, two paint thinner, and one turpentine. The lacquer thinner is for cleaning the brushes and palette, the paint thinner for blending colors and mixing washes, and the turpentine for thinning the paints in their tins. I cover the table with newspaper so I can wipe paintbrushes on it, and use facial tissue for general cleanup.

A glass dental palette about ½" thick is used to mix the paints. The paint is stirred (never shaken) in the tins with a polished wire about $\frac{1}{16}$" in diameter, and this stirring rod is used to transfer the paint to the glass. I like Winsor &

Newton Series 33 brushes for general painting and Series 7 No. 000 for fine detail. I keep an Optivisor (a binocular magnifier worn on the head) handy for painting fine detail.

My figures are painted under normal studio lighting, although I realize that colored lights may eventually be used in the scene, which may cause problems — yellow may appear white under a yellow light.

A philosophy of figure painting. My method of painting figures is unorthodox, but it works for me. I start by painting the figure with opaque highlight colors (the lightest tint of the color that will appear on the figure), then use a series of transparent washes in the shadows to add depth. This flies in the face of conventional figure-painting wisdom, but it allows me to finish many figures in a short time because the Humbrol colors dry quickly.

In a way this approach is similar to the techniques used by the old masters to achieve depth in their paintings. When looking at a face, note the highlight on the bridge of the nose. It is opaque, not transparent — a bit of solid color. Now look at the eyes and note the shadows around them. They are trans-

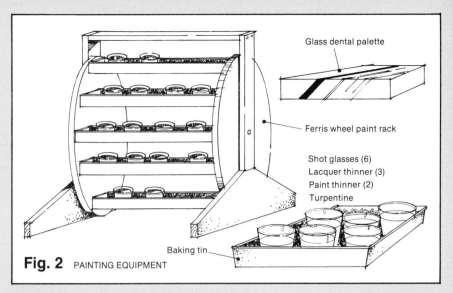

Fig. 2 PAINTING EQUIPMENT

Glass dental palette

Ferris wheel paint rack

Shot glasses (6)
Lacquer thinner (3)
Paint thinner (2)
Turpentine

Baking tin

Fig. 3. This unusual (and irreverent) subject, a Southern California beachfront street scene, shows how Ray lightens and grays even colorful clothing. Also note how the colors have been shaded with darker washes of the same hues.

Fig. 4. In one of Ray's western dioramas, "Justice," a traveling judge is holding court in the saloon. The patent medicine salesman in the center of the scene is accused of responsibility for the condition of the young lady on the right. Study the variety of colors in the blue clothing on the man at the left of the scene.

parent colors with the basic skin tones showing through.

I try to duplicate this on the figures. I first underpaint the figure with the highlight colors and let them dry. Next, I add washes of the darker colors; each succeeding wash is a little darker and is applied to the deeper crevices. The washes may be of slightly different colors. For example, a light blue skirt may have a slightly pink wash to break up the basic color. A thin yellow wash will help a plain green. In a few cases it's necessary to dry-brush highlights after the deeper shades have been added.

Lightening and graying colors. Although many figures in my dioramas wear relatively bright-colored outfits, if you study the photos carefully, you'll find that the color content of clothing is actually low-key, Fig. 3. This is intentional, because reducing the brilliance of the colors increases the realism of the overall scene.

In some cases reducing the strength of the colors means adding white, but more often I gray down the color some other way. Lightening a color by merely adding white can result in a disagreeably weak tint, and a better way to reduce intensity is to add either the complement of the color or a neutral gray.

Let's take a typical blue jacket on a figure in one of my western scenes, Fig. 4, as an example of painting technique. Instead of an opaque, uniform denim

Fig. 5. Look hard at the colors in the shadows of "Perry's Creek, Fourth of July," and you'll find that most shadows are transparent, allowing the underlying color to show through. Even the sooty interior of the blacksmith shop includes brown and blue, not dead black.

blue, we'll start by mixing a faded blue, with a hint of green, and painting that on the figure. Then we add darker blue washes to deepen the color in the folds and shadows.

On top of the intentionally lightened and faded colors I add washes to represent dirt and grime. When completed, our "simple" blue jacket will, upon close inspection, include hints of seven or eight colors. I can't stress this enough: Try to get away from just one color, because single colors are dull. Pure colors are seldom found in nature, and varying both color and intensity will make your figures more alive.

Dark washes — but never black. I use dark, transparent washes in the shadows, but it's important to add that I never use black. Black masks the opaque color beneath it, muddying the shadows and dulling the underlying colors. Instead, I use a dark wash of the highlight color: dark blue, dark brown, dark gray, and so on, Fig. 5.

I try to make the shadows on the figures correspond to the cast shadows in the scene. If the lighting is overhead, the shadows will radiate downward such as the shadow under the nose. If the figure is on a stage with footlights shining up, the highlight will be under the nose and the shadow on the bridge. As the distance of the figures increases from the front of the scene, they should be painted with less color content and softer shadows.

Years ago I wanted to portray sooty stonework on a church interior (page 24). When I added black to the highlight color, it came out dull and lifeless — and trying again yielded the same results. I woke up one night wondering if a dark blue would work instead of the black. It did! To my surprise it added life and depth to the piece. After consulting "experts" I found there is no such color as true black. There are dark blues, greens, and so on, but no black. All ordinary shadows should have some color content.

Suggesting distance with color. Although we can paint a single figure with a bright red tunic, perhaps with a touch of yellow to increase the color intensity, add white pants, and come up with a pleasing result when the figure is mounted on a base, we shouldn't do the same for a diorama figure. Why not? Well, when a single figure is on a base, it's a statue, and there's no need for it to relate to anything around it. But when the figure is part of a diorama, it's a different ball game.

In a diorama, where objects (including figures) are at different distances from the viewer, their apparent colors should differ. As objects are moved further from the viewer the dark colors appear lighter and the light colors seem to darken, while all colors tend more toward neutral grays.

If our soldier figure is in the foreground, close to the viewer, the red will

be toned down only slightly and the white pants will darken just a little. If the figure is further back in the scene, the red will be considerably less bright, and the pants darker yet. At the back of the scene both garments will be a medium tan-gray with just a touch of red in the tunic and white in the pants. By reducing bright colors almost to gray, we add depth and realism to the scene.

Warm colors (reds and oranges) make objects seem closer; cool colors (blues and greens) make them seem further away, so most often we'll add cold colors to help suggest distance. Nature's grays are seldom neutral; some color must appear in them. I find cold tan works in western scenes, while blue is better for mountain scenes.

While on the subject of suggesting distance, I should add that the edges of distance details should be softened, and the depth of shadows reduced. Green is one of my favorite colors to give the feeling of depth.

Our next installment will cover one of my favorite aspects of diorama building: the outer case. See you then. **FSM**

27

Converting Historex soldiers — into just about anything!

Step-by-step techniques for posing and detailing plastic figures

BY RAY ANDERSON / PHOTOS BY ROLAND PATTERSON

CONVERTING PLASTIC figures is easy — easier than working with soft metal, epoxy putty, or Sculpey. Thanks mostly to the availability of the Historex line of 54 mm Napoleonic figures and parts, I've converted almost a thousand figures since 1972, most of them for use in over 100 boxed dioramas. In this article I'll share my simple techniques with you.

About Historex figures. Historex, a French firm, has offered 54 mm Napoleonic soldiers and supporting charac-

ters for roughly 20 years. The figure kits are molded in white styrene and are multi-part: Heads, torsos, arms, and leg pairs are separate items. The extensive line includes many accessories, as well as interesting and useful spare parts such as hands and crossed legs.

I obtain individual parts from Historex Agents in England rather than purchasing complete kits. When choosing parts, I specify gaitered legs, because they require less shaping than

legs with full pants, and beardless heads for much the same reason. The "Academy" female nudes are excellent for converting to children, and there are also some children figures available. The male "Academy" nudes are rather poorly done, but can be used for background figures.

With determination and ingenuity it's possible to alter Historex components to model any of the peoples of the world. Once you have a little experience it's even possible to create a specific person. I've been asked to re-create family incidents with figures copied

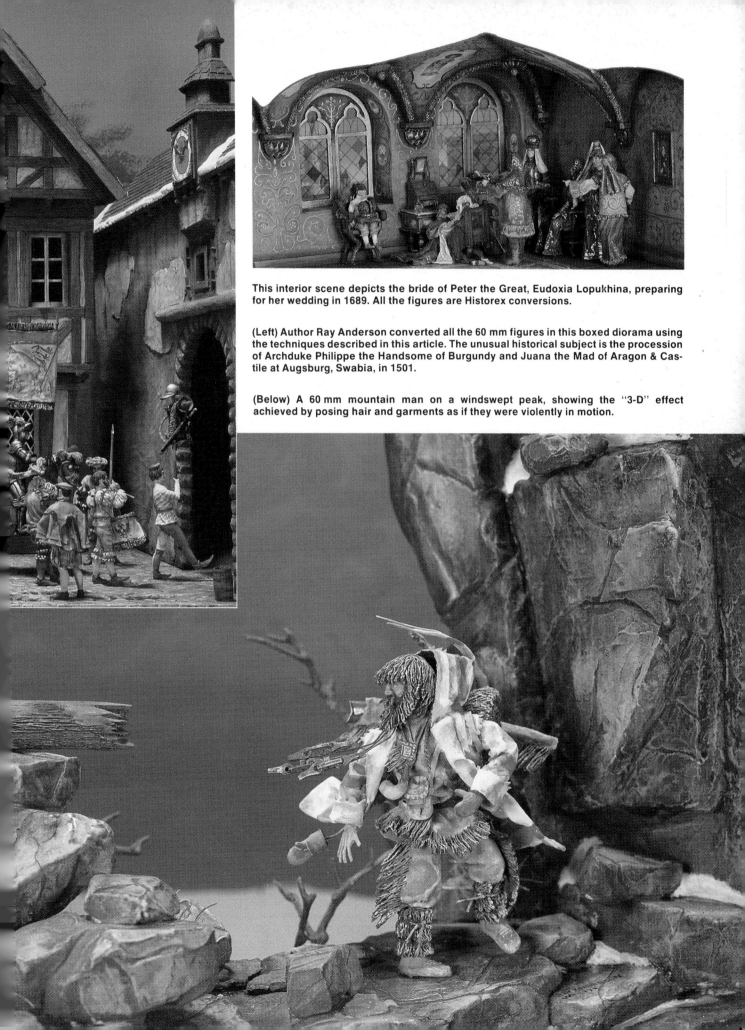

This interior scene depicts the bride of Peter the Great, Eudoxia Lopukhina, preparing for her wedding in 1689. All the figures are Historex conversions.

(Left) Author Ray Anderson converted all the 60 mm figures in this boxed diorama using the techniques described in this article. The unusual historical subject is the procession of Archduke Philippe the Handsome of Burgundy and Juana the Mad of Aragon & Castile at Augsburg, Swabia, in 1501.

(Below) A 60 mm mountain man on a windswept peak, showing the "3-D" effect achieved by posing hair and garments as if they were violently in motion.

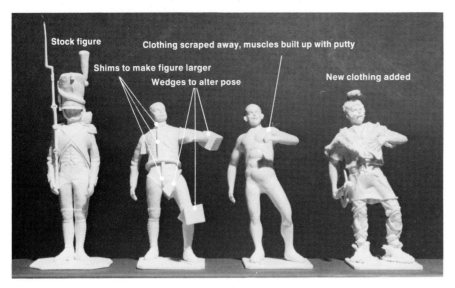

Stock figure

Clothing scraped away, muscles built up with putty

Shims to make figure larger

Wedges to alter pose

New clothing added

Fig. 1. From left to right, a stock Historex 54 mm foot soldier becomes a fierce, fur-clad axeman. The head, shown here finished on the nude figure, is usually added to the torso and detailed after the clothing has been built up.

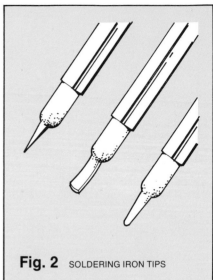

Fig. 2 SOLDERING IRON TIPS

Figures for the Augsburg diorama (page 28) before painting. Note the variety of clothing, and the way the light from behind shows through the thin, plastic-coated tissue.

A samurai of the Kuki clan, Edo Period. This 75 mm conversion from Historex components represents the upper limit to which these figures can be stretched.

from old family albums — one of my clients always wanted to play the role of a madame in the old west, and in 60 mm scale, she does!

Although I won't discuss anatomy here, concentrating instead on the mechanics of creating the figures, a good book on anatomy is an essential reference. Study the book until you understand body proportions for both sexes and for all ages. (One good test for the "flow," or balance, of a figure is whether it will stand by itself.)

The basic approach. Figure 1 illustrates the basic conversion technique. I cut, shim, and wedge the Historex parts to create and pose the figure, then remove uniform detail and surplus plastic with files and a modeling knife. The musculature and facial features are built up with a homemade

putty consisting of dissolved plastic scraps. I dress the nude figure with clothing made of facial tissue coated with dissolved plastic, and add fur and hair textures with a fine soldering iron tip.

My figures are 60 mm scale, where 60 mm equals roughly 6 feet. To me, the standard 54 mm Historex scale is uncomfortable to work with, so I've adopted the slightly bigger size. It's just enough larger to allow substantially more detail.

The only disadvantage of plastic is that the solvent must be allowed to evaporate after each application, so it can take several weeks to sculpt and clothe a figure. Because of this I work on many figures — up to 50 — at the same time. Although the work is spread over several weeks, the time spent on

an average figure works out to about four hours.

Materials and tools. The putty for building up the figures consists of styrene scraps dissolved in trichloroethylene, which of all the plastic solvents I've tried has the best viscosity and evaporation rate. I also use this solvent as my plastic cement. Like many solvents, trichloroethylene is toxic and should be used in a well-ventilated area. I have a small desk fan about a foot from my workplace to pull the fumes away.

You'll need three 2-ounce bottles with varying proportions of sprue to solvent. The first bottle is for initially dissolving styrene scraps in the solvent to make a plastic "stock," which is thinned further for use. The thinned putty in the second bottle is for coating

Note the variety of poses and dress possibile in these 60 mm figures. These are Haida Indians for Ray's diorama, *The Coming of the Killer Whale People* (see pages 20 and 21).

tissue clothing and should be the consistency of milk. The third mix is thicker, just thin enough that it will not make strings when lifted with a brush; this is for building up muscles and hair.

The figures are built up by applying the thicker putty with a brush, not unlike adding muscles to a skeleton. You'll need a small file or knife on occasion, but most of the sculpting is done by adding material with brushes. Designate several inexpensive brushes for this, and trim one down to about 1/64" diameter for fine details such as ears. You'll also need a slightly larger brush for nose and lip detail, and a No. 3 or 4 brush for applying the thinned putty over clothing. Dental tools can be

used to reposition the putty once a surface skin has formed.

A 15-watt soldering iron with interchangeable tips is the last tool you'll need. The paddle tip shown in Fig. 2 is useful for adding larger quantities of styrene to the figure, and the fine tips are for texturing. A temperature regulator may also be necessary [See "Detailing plastic — with heat," March/April 1986 FSM]. I also use the small fan near my workbench to pull the plastic fumes away when using the soldering iron.

Getting started. The most important advantage of working with plastic figures is that they can be posed *exactly* the way you want them. Never compromise your design concept by trying to

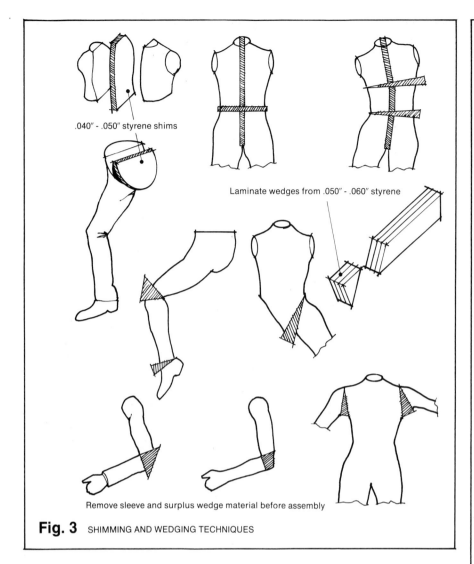

.040″ - .050″ styrene shims

Laminate wedges from .050″ - .060″ styrene

Remove sleeve and surplus wedge material before assembly

Fig. 3   SHIMMING AND WEDGING TECHNIQUES

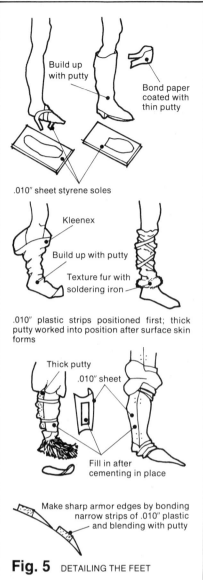

Build up with putty

Bond paper coated with thin putty

.010″ sheet styrene soles

Kleenex

Build up with putty

Texture fur with soldering iron

.010″ plastic strips positioned first; thick putty worked into position after surface skin forms

Thick putty

.010″ sheet

Fill in after cementing in place

Make sharp armor edges by bonding narrow strips of .010″ plastic and blending with putty

Fig. 5   DETAILING THE FEET

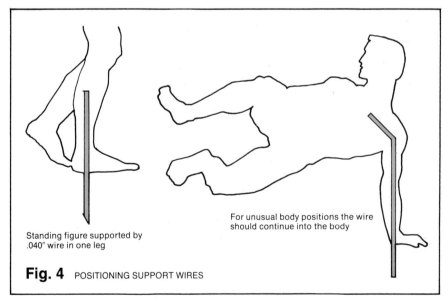

Standing figure supported by .040″ wire in one leg

For unusual body positions the wire should continue into the body

Fig. 4   POSITIONING SUPPORT WIRES

use existing parts; instead, modify the parts to fit your requirements. (Incidentally, given this philosophy you can start with virtually any components.)

To be correctly proportioned for the larger 60 mm scale the Historex figures must be made both taller and wider, so start by adding a .050″ styrene shim between the legs (I purchase styrene in large sheets from a plastic supply house — see your Yellow Pages). Halve the upper body with a razor saw,

Fig. 3, and add another .050″ shim. Let these joints dry overnight, then remove surplus material. If the figure is to stand upright add a third .050″ shim to the bottom of the torso; if the upper body will tilt use a wedge instead.

When this assembly has dried overnight, start repositioning the legs. The cutting and wedging techniques shown in Fig. 3 are essential to ensure that body joints fall in the right places. Make diagonal cuts at the hips first, then reposition the knees and ankles before reattaching the legs to the torso. Attach one leg at a time and let each joint dry overnight. Don't fret if a body component is not the right length or in the correct position when first assembled — it's easy to cut the figure apart and make corrections after the joints have dried.

When the assembled body and legs have dried overnight remove surplus material with an X-Acto knife and files. File the bottoms of the feet flat,

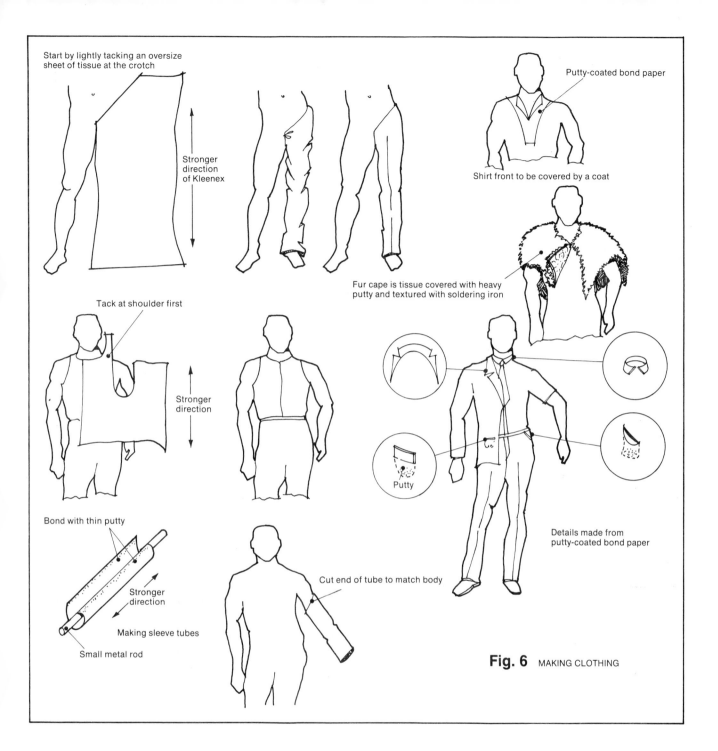

Start by lightly tacking an oversize sheet of tissue at the crotch

Stronger direction of Kleenex

Putty-coated bond paper

Shirt front to be covered by a coat

Fur cape is tissue covered with heavy putty and textured with soldering iron

Tack at shoulder first

Stronger direction

Bond with thin putty

Putty

Stronger direction

Small metal rod

Making sleeve tubes

Cut end of tube to match body

Details made from putty-coated bond paper

Fig. 6 MAKING CLOTHING

drill a hole up into one leg, and cement in a length of .040″ wire, Fig. 4. If the figure will be posed standing on one foot, use larger wire.

Figure 4 also shows how to support a figure that will be mounted in an unusual position. Embed an .040″ or larger support wire securely in the shoulder by cutting a groove up the back of the arm and shoulder with a small round saw mounted in a motor tool. The groove must be deep enough that the wire will not project beyond the surface. Coat the wire with thick putty when you install it, and after the putty has dried fill the cavity with plastic scraps using the soldering iron.

Adding the head and arms. Trim the collar, ears, and surplus material from the Historex head and add a .020″ shim to the bottom of the neck. If the mouth is to be open, drill a .040″ hole below the upper lip and widen it into an oblong shape with a knife. It is easier to do this while the head is separate. Another technique is to open the mouth cavity with the small tip on the soldering iron, which also partially forms lips. After cementing the head to the body and allowing the joint to dry, remove the surplus shim and blend the neck with a small rattail file. You can start to build up the neck with putty at this point; the neck should be com-

pleted before you start to add clothing.

Select arms and wedge the elbows if necessary; when dry, trim away the sleeves and surplus wedge material. Make sure the upper body width is correct before adding the arms. This completes the basic figure.

Muscle building. The next phase is building up the muscle structure. It need not be finely detailed except where the skin is exposed or where the way clothing is draped will reflect the muscles underneath, such as the upper surface of an extended leg. A combination of trimming, filing, and puttying is required.

Build up the calves, thighs, rump,

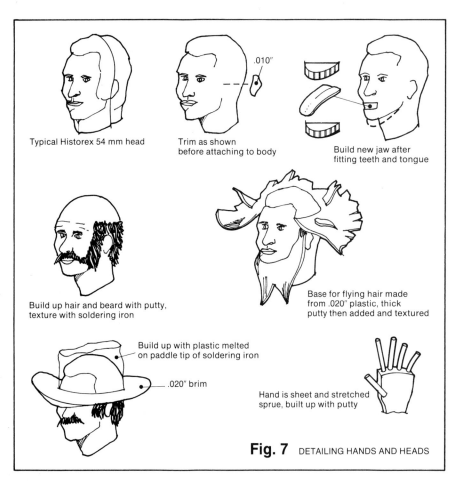

Typical Historex 54 mm head

Trim as shown before attaching to body

.010″

Build new jaw after fitting teeth and tongue

Build up hair and beard with putty, texture with soldering iron

Base for flying hair made from .020″ plastic, thick putty then added and textured

Build up with plastic melted on paddle tip of soldering iron

.020″ brim

Hand is sheet and stretched sprue, built up with putty

Fig. 7 DETAILING HANDS AND HEADS

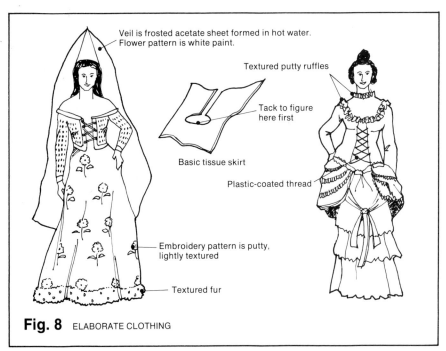

Veil is frosted acetate sheet formed in hot water. Flower pattern is white paint.

Textured putty ruffles

Tack to figure here first

Basic tissue skirt

Plastic-coated thread

Embroidery pattern is putty, lightly textured

Textured fur

Fig. 8 ELABORATE CLOTHING

shoulders, and back of the head, but never add more than $\frac{1}{32}$″ of putty at a time and always allow it to dry overnight. There is always a tendency to add too much putty at one time, but keep in mind that coats thicker than $\frac{1}{32}$″ simply won't harden. Where you need thicker sections, build them up with chunks of plastic or add plastic melted with the soldering iron tip.

Once the body is roughed in, finish the feet, Fig. 5. For bare feet it's easiest to add a small block for the big toe and trim it to size; the rest of the toes can be carved from the built-up foot. For shoes, finish the uppers first, then add .010″ sheet soles.

Kleenex for clothing. The clothing is Kleenex facial tissue. Its rough texture requires several coats of putty to cover, but the tissue must be strong enough to withstand shrinkage as the solvent in the thinned putty evaporates. I've found Kleenex is stronger in one direction than the other, and the stronger direction should run the length of the arm, leg, or torso.

Start with the pants, Fig. 6. Cut the tissue oversize and trim to size on the figure. Lightly tack a swatch of tissue in the front crotch with thinned putty, and when it has set, drape the front of the pant leg to mid calf. Coat the tissue with thinned putty and hold it for a few seconds until the solvent evaporates. Slowly work around the leg, draping and coating as you go. Place the seam out of sight, perhaps between the legs.

The first clothing contours are not final, because the tissue can be softened and redraped by moistening it with solvent. When you're satisfied with the draping and trimming give the leg a second coat of thin putty to stiffen it so the other leg can be started. The tissue will shrink slightly as the putty dries. When both legs are finished, brush on two or three coats of thinned putty to eliminate the tissue grain. Don't add more putty than necessary, because it tends to smooth out the folds.

Shirts and coats. When a coat or vest will cover the shirt make only the shirt front. An open shirt front can be made from bond paper coated with thin putty. Figure 6 shows a full shirt cut from Kleenex. Start by tacking a shoulder strip, then work your way around the body — I usually make the shirt in two pieces joined at the back. The shirt should overhang where the belt will be added, and it adds interest if a button is missing and there is a gap in the shirt front. The way the fabric drapes can be altered by moistening the putty with solvent after the first coat or two, and it helps to moisten the tweezers or dental tools used for reshaping. Make collars, pockets, and other clothing details from plastic-coated bond paper.

For sleeves, first make tubes by wrapping Kleenex around a metal rod. The tubes are tricky to make, and they should be removed from the wire rod while the putty remains tacky. If the hands will require extensive modification or if extended fingers will get in the way, cut off the hands before slipping the sleeve onto the arm. Trim the top of the tube at an angle to match the body, and locate the seam of the tube where it will have to flex the least at the elbow. Tack the sleeve at the shoulder and when the tack has set push the sleeve up the arm to obtain realistic folds, then coat with putty.

Detailing the head. Except for details such as collars and buttons I usually finish dressing the figure before detailing the head. Because the clothing adds bulk to the figure, it's easier to sculpt the proper head proportions with the clothing in place. Once the solvent has evaporated the putty-coated clothing is stiff and will stand considerable abuse — such as dropping the figure.

If the mouth is to be open, flatten the top and bottom surfaces to accept .020″ styrene teeth, Fig. 7. Insert the upper teeth first, then the tongue, then the lower teeth — omitting one front tooth makes for an interesting effect. Next build up a new lower jaw, roughing it in with the soldering iron and finishing with putty. Make lips from beads of putty, coaxing them into position after a skin has formed. This provides realistic gaps between teeth and lips.

Cut ears from .010″ sheet and cement them to the head at an angle. Add ear details with putty applied with a fine brush. Historex heads are undersize for 60 mm, so build up the back and top with putty. A book on cartooning is a helpful reference for creating facial expressions — each face should have a distinct personality, depending upon the role the figure will play for you.

Hats, hair, hands, and the fair sex. I make hat brims from .020″ sheet, Fig. 7, giving them two or three coats of solvent (allowing the surface to dry after each coat) to make them flexible. Then the brim is positioned on the head and shaping completed. Build up the hat crown with the soldering iron.

Build up hair and beards from putty. Make basic forms for flying hair from .020″ sheet, softened with thinner. After the solvent dries, trim the ends and add slivers of plastic at an angle to the base, then build up with putty. Flying hair suggests movement and adds an extra touch of three-dimensional effect.

The hands are fragile, so work with them last. Make free-standing fingers from stretched sprue, then build up with putty. When the hands are complete, so is your figure.

Before I close, a few thoughts on modeling the fairer sex are in order. The female nude Academy figures can easily be converted; for plumper figures, start with males. Shape skirts from squares of Kleenex, and once you've got some experience under your belt, try your hand at elaborately dressed ladies, Fig. 8. Although they may look fancy, converting them requires only repeated application of the techniques described above. **FSM**

SOURCES

• Historex figures and parts are available from Santos Miniatures, P. O. Box 4062, Harrisburg, PA 17111, and Historex Agents, 3 Castle Street, Dover, Kent, UK CT16 1QJ, England.

Another view of the unpainted figures for the Augsburg diorama. The wide variety of poses and clothing demonstrates the flexibility of the techniques.

All 26 (that's right, twenty-six!) figures in this *Rus Funeral Pyre* diorama were made using Historex parts, not to mention the cow and two horses.

A closeup of two key figures from the Augsburg scene. Note the extremely fine detail on the fringe of the horse blanket and on the drummer's breeches and leggings.

Among the most elaborate of Ray's outer case treatments is "Venezia," a Venice canal scene. The frame was covered with genuine 23-carat gold leaf, then abraded, allowing the red under-coating to show through to establish an authentically old look.

The art of the diorama

Part 5: Outer case design, construction, and finishing

(Right) "Criterion" shows how a California coast town might look after the great earthquake and resulting submergence. One of Ray's most unusual boxes, the case and frame designs help emphasize the shape and the subject matter.

BY RAY ANDERSON
PHOTOS BY ROLAND PATTERSON

PRESENTATION is always an important aspect of storytelling, and in a boxed diorama presentation means packaging. The packaging, needless to say, is the outer box, or case.

When I first began building boxed dioramas I didn't place much emphasis on the outer cases, and as a result their quality didn't equal what was inside them. In fact, I had an unfounded concern that elaborate cases might detract from key features in the scenes themselves.

It soon became apparent that the opposite is true: The case is an integral part of the scene, and it must enhance and support the story we are trying to tell inside it. A good scene deserves an attractive package, and anything less may detract from its impact.

Cases that look the part. One way to reinforce the effect we're out to establish with the box as a whole is to try to have the case look as if it comes from the same period as the scene. By aging the cases with nicks, cracks, and worm holes, applying gold leaf, or simulating the reliquaries used to store religious objects in medieval times, we can help our viewer imagine (and believe) that he's looking into a three-dimensional story from an earlier time. We'll get to the techniques for such treatments in a few minutes, after we talk about building the basic box.

Building the shell. The procedure for determining the dimensions of the outer case was discussed in detail in part 2 of this series. I use birch-faced, mahogany-core 5 mm plywood for the shell and most of the parts, Fig. 1. Imported from Taiwan, this material is usually used for door skins, and while it is relatively expensive, its smooth surface and flatness simplify construction and finishing.

Most of the strength of such plywood is in the core, so the grain of the core should run in the direction of the long dimension of each part. With some noteworthy exceptions, my outer cases are similar to Fig. 1, and cutting the plywood parts in the sequence shown both saves time and results in a precise box. I use a table saw, and even an inexpensive Sears hollow-ground blade will yield a fine, precise cut. (As with any fine work, double check the accuracy of the miter guide and fence before cutting.)

The box should be reinforced at the corners to keep it square. I assemble the shell with wood glue and ¾" No. 20 brads after pre-drilling the nail holes on a drill press. Then I recess the nail heads and fill all the holes.

Using laminate and veneer coverings. If the case is to be covered with a plastic laminate, select something that is compatible with the scene. My preference is for simulated wood grain laminates, and there are some beautiful, realistic grain patterns available. If you can, select a single piece of laminate long enough that the grain pattern can run up one side of the shell, continue across the top, and down the

This box, "Male Shooting Chant, Navajo," includes a complex, double-molding front frame with Indian paintings in the matted area. Ray finishes each box so that it may be displayed comfortably even in rooms with formal furnishings.

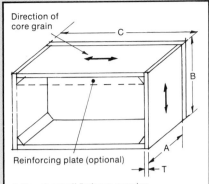

Fig. 1 BASIC BOX CONSTRUCTION

Direction of core grain

Reinforcing plate (optional)

1. Rough cut all 5 pieces oversize
2. Cut top, bottom, and sides to dimension A using table saw and fence
3. Set fence to dimension B, cut sides and back
4. Cut back to dimension C
5. Set fence to dimension C-2T, cut top, bottom, and (if used) reinforcing plate

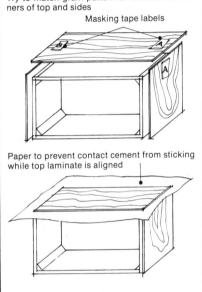

Try to match grain pattern of laminate at corners of top and sides

Masking tape labels

Paper to prevent contact cement from sticking while top laminate is aligned

Fig. 2 APPLYING PLASTIC LAMINATE

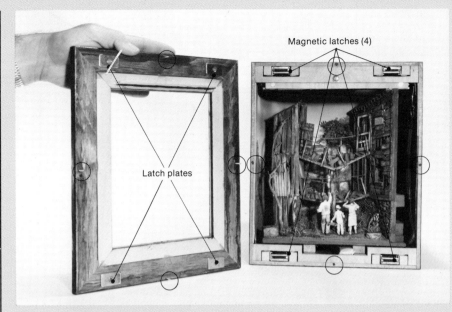

Fig. 3. A typical boxed diorama with the front frame removed. Four magnetic cabinet latches hold the frame securely against the unfinished front edge of the box; four pins (circled) fit into holes in the box to provide positive alignment. A. L. Schmidt photo.

Magnetic latches (4)

Latch plates

opposite side, Fig. 2. This looks best.

Bonding and edging the laminate is a simple process, particularly if you have a router equipped with a straight carbide laminate cutter. (Lacking a router, most carpenters can do the job for you.) Using an old saw blade, rip the laminate about 1″ wider than the box — for your first attempt, cut the sides and top with about 1″ surplus each. Use masking tape labels with pencil notes to identify which laminate edges must be matched.

Next, clean the box surface with a tack rag, then coat the two sides of the shell and the backs of the sheets of laminate that will be applied to them with GRIP contact cement. This is a critical step, because we don't want the bond to

loosen at some future time. I recommend GRIP because it has never failed me, but Constantine (listed below) also offers an excellent contact cement.

When the cement is dry to the touch, bond the laminate to the shell. Remember, with contact cement you have only one chance at alignment — the panels can't be moved once contact has been made. Place one panel on a table, glue side up, and carefully press the box shell onto it. Hold a block of wood against the surface of the laminate and tap it with a hammer to ensure solid contact and bonding.

Clamp the box to your workbench to trim the laminate, then clean off all loose particles and apply contact cement to the top and the laminate for it.

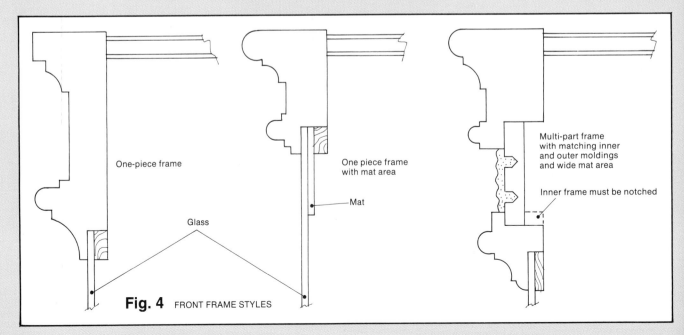

One-piece frame

Glass

One piece frame with mat area

Mat

Multi-part frame with matching inner and outer moldings and wide mat area

Inner frame must be notched

Fig. 4 FRONT FRAME STYLES

The next step is a little tricky, because we want approximately an equal overhang on each side, and we want to have the grain patterns aligned at both edges. When the contact cement has dried, position a sheet of smooth paper on the shell, then align the laminate on top of it, Fig. 2. When you're satisfied with the fit, slowly withdraw the paper, allow the contact cement to bond, and follow up with the wood block and hammer. After using the router to trim the top edges, I paint the backs of my cases flat black and cover the bottoms with thin felt.

An alternative to plastic laminate is real wood veneer. Albert Constantine and Son (see sources, below) offers many attractive veneers, and their thin, paper-backed veneers are as easy to apply as the plastic laminates (and don't require a router). Constantine also offers excellent reference books and all the materials to do the job right.

The front frame. Once the outer case is veneered, precise dimensions for the front frame can be established. The frame should be flush with the bottom of the case and extend 1/16″ to 1/8″ beyond the sides and top, to cover the front raw edge of the case, Fig. 3.

My typical front frame is from 2″ to 3″ wide — often 2½″ — and there are three basic designs, Fig. 4. The frame can be one piece, which can be expensive if a wide frame is required, or you can use a frame with a mat, either inside or outside the glass. The third configuration, and the most complicated, consists of inner and outer frames with a matted space between, Fig. 5. The inner and outer frame moldings must be compatible for such a treatment, and the back of the inner frame must be notched to accept the mat area, which can be filled with all sorts of interesting materials.

Some of my most interesting front frames have the matted area filled with Durham's Water Putty (see part 3 of this series). For a scene of ancient southwest cliff dwellers, a hard stone finish was used in the mat area and ancient hieroglyphics were scratched into the Durham's. A red putty covered with an earth-colored powder was used for a number of scenes. Typical Indian designs can be cut into the red base. Indian pictographs have been used to tell the story of the scene, and I've used various cattle brands on a cowboy scene. My box depicting the burial of Dirty Dora, the madame of Lone Pine, even has her Boot Hill epitaph inscribed on the frame!

Scenes from the medieval and renaissance periods will be enhanced if front frames appropriate to the time are used. The Italian Renaissance frame shown on page 36 is particularly at-

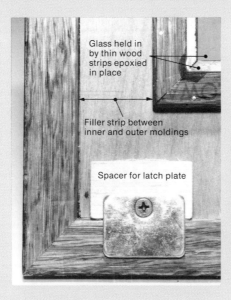

Fig. 5. A close-up of the back corner of a complicated frame. Note the filler used to connect the two moldings, and how the glass is fastened. A. L. Schmidt photo.

Glass held in by thin wood strips epoxied in place

Filler strip between inner and outer moldings

Spacer for latch plate

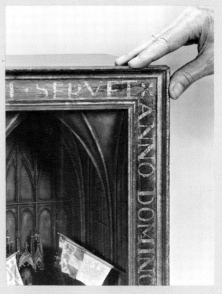

Fig. 6. Lettering (here, in Latin) in the mat area of a frame can help tell the story or simply provide atmosphere.

tractive in that it includes its own perspective treatment to lead the viewer into the scene. Another interesting style incorporates lettering in the mat area, Fig. 6.

In recent years it has been increasingly difficult to find wood frame materials that can be adapted to these styles. I've had to strip old frames, then modify them, or combine portions of different materials. The moldings can, of course, be produced from scratch if you have woodworking skills and the right equipment, which includes a table saw and hand tools such as a Record multi-plane or an old Stanley molding plane.

About gold leaf. To establish an authentic period look, several of my frames have incorporated gold leaf. I prefer real gold leaf to the synthetic variety, because it won't tarnish (as the synthetic will do) but is not much more expensive. The synthetics and 22-carat real gold have a cold, brassy appearance; in contrast, my favorite product, Giusto Manetti XX Deep Glass 23-carat gold, yields a warm, pleasing

Fig. 7. The frame of this Indian diorama is heavily distressed, and includes carefully rendered peeling paint to convey the feeling of age and weather. The pictograms on the frame tell the story of the three squaws and their journey.

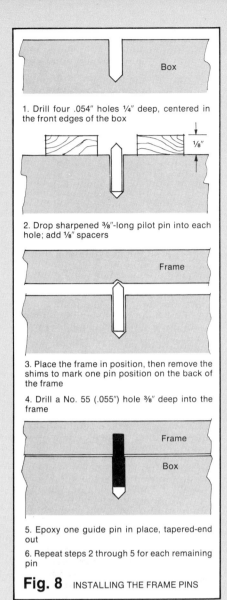

1. Drill four .054" holes ¼" deep, centered in the front edges of the box

2. Drop sharpened ⅜"-long pilot pin into each hole; add ⅛" spacers

3. Place the frame in position, then remove the shims to mark one pin position on the back of the frame

4. Drill a No. 55 (.055") hole ⅜" deep into the frame

5. Epoxy one guide pin in place, tapered-end out

6. Repeat steps 2 through 5 for each remaining pin

Fig. 8   INSTALLING THE FRAME PINS

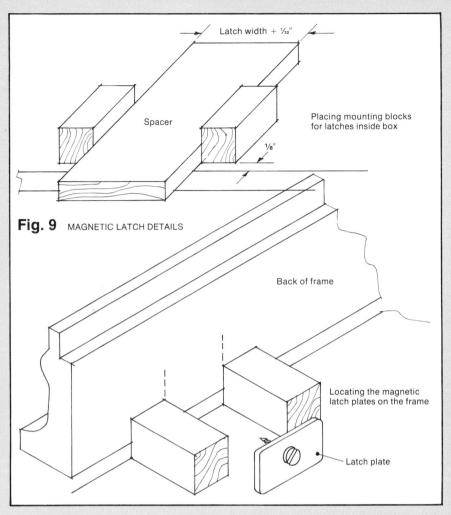

Fig. 9   MAGNETIC LATCH DETAILS

color. (I don't know if the difference is due to the added karat, or because the leaf is thinner, allowing more of the red undercoat to show through.)

I use "wind" or "patent" gold leaf, which comes lightly attached to a backing paper, simplifying handling. To find it in your area, call paint supply houses that cater to sign painters. *Gold Leaf Techniques* (listed below) is a useful guidebook. I substitute a smooth red paint under the gold for the red clay bole and rabbit-skin glue used in medieval times. *The Materials and Techniques of Medieval Painting* (also listed below), has all the techniques used during that period. To bond the leaf to the base I use a slow-drying, high-adhesion varnish, which yields a smooth, attractive gold finish.

Aging the frames. Distressing the frame, Fig. 7, helps authenticate the box — and ultimately, the scene. Close examination of old frames in museums will show you how. Often the gold leaf will be worn, exposing the red clay bole

beneath; you can duplicate this effect with very fine steel wool. The bole will be chipped at the corner miters, and there will be other dings and chips. One professional frame shop I visit uses a heavy chain on the frames to duplicate the dings, and they even add worm holes!

The possible treatments for the frame are nearly endless — for example, you can add flat earth tones in cracks and corners to simulate accumulations of dust and dirt. There's a great deal of smug satisfaction to be had from seeing a frame age several hundred years in a few days, but be aware that the whole business can be overdone, so proceed cautiously, and when in doubt study real frames.

Attaching the frame to the box. The next challenge is to neatly mount the front frame to the outer case without exposed fasteners. I've tried several methods, but have settled on a standard combination of four magnetic latches and guide pins, Fig. 3. High-quality magnetic cabinet latches (about 79 cents each) are the ones to use, because some of the cheaper brands don't provide the the necessary magnetic strength to hold the frame securely against the box.

I use four ⅝"-long guide pins made from No. 17 wire nails to positively align the frame to the box, Fig, 8. The magnetic latches are screwed to small wood blocks cemented into the outer case, Fig. 3, and a small scrap of plywood 1/32" wider than the latch will ensure the proper spacing of the blocks when gluing, Fig. 9. Mount the frame on the shell and mark the location of the latch blocks and the inner edge on the frame. These marks will establish where to attach the metal latch plates so they'll clear the outer case when the box is assembled.

Install the magnetic latches loosely, then reach through the frame opening to tighten the screws. With a small mirror check that all four latches are seated against their plates; there should be a little clearance between the frame and case to allow some air circulation and to ensure that the latches will seat properly. It's a good idea to mark the final location of the latches as they cannot be adjusted after the frame glass is in place.

Glass comes last. The last step in building the outer box is to install the glass, and at that point, you're done. In the next issue we'll once again step *inside* the box, to discuss the imporant

40

"After 93 days on the Chisholm" is typical of Ray's old west dioramas. This one includes a heavy wood frame to evoke the rough-and-tumble nature of cowboy life.

subject of diorama lighting. **FSM**

REFERENCES

- LeBlanc, Raymond J., *Gold Leaf Techniques*, Signs of the Times Publishing Co., Cincinnati, 1980
- Thompson, Daniel V., *The Materials and Techniques of Medieval Painting*, Dover Press, ISBN 0-486-20327, 1956.

SOURCES

- Veneer and workworking supplies, Albert Constantine and Son, Inc., 2050 Eastchester Road, Bronx, NY 10461
- GRIP contact cement, Indal Aluminum Products, Los Angeles, CA

Although Ray's text describes how to build and finish a typical diorama box, that's not the only kind he builds. (Below left) "The Swamp," a fantasy scene, is housed in a wild outer case that portrays a ruined jungle idol. Those eyes in the upper portion of the box scan from side to side — this box looks back at you! (Right) Just for fun, Ray built a "Stealth Bomber" diorama, and housed it in an old TV set case. Look hard and you'll see the ultimate in stealth: Two pilots flying an utterly invisible plane!

The art of the diorama

Part 6: Lighting boxed dioramas

BY RAY ANDERSON

PHOTOS BY ROLAND PATTERSON

LIGHTING DIORAMAS IS FUN, because with comparatively little effort we can establish or alter the mood of a scene, much in the way that stage lighting can influence a theater audience. And like the theater we can employ a full range of lighting colors and techniques, from simulating the cold blue light of a high mountain range to replicating the brilliant reds and oranges of the Southwest.

The cardinal rule. Before we delve into techniques I want to state one cardinal rule for lighting boxed dioramas: The scene lighting must be more powerful than the overall room lighting where the diorama is displayed. This is so important that, in an instance where we know where the piece will ultimately be displayed, the room lighting may even influence the choice of subject for the box.

You'll remember that in any boxed diorama we want a large front opening so the story being told "surrounds" and involves the viewer. A large front opening means the scene can be enjoyed — or at least glimpsed — from across the room, and we also want, whenever possible, to bring the action up to the glass. For all these reasons we'll need enough light inside the box to overpower the room lighting outside it. Beginners tend to skimp on the scene lighting, but it's better by far to err on the side of making the scene too bright.

Incandescent or fluorescent? So, how do we shoehorn lots of light into an enclosure that's only about one foot on a side? There's more than one answer, of course, including exotic (and expensive) types of lighting, but for most of us the choice comes down to the two common types of 110-volt household lighting, incandescent and fluorescent. Both types are available in sizes small enough to fit in our boxes.

While either incandescent or fluorescent lighting can be used (and Shep Paine provides an excellent explanation of incandescent lighting in his book, *How to Build Dioramas*), I use fluorescents in most of my scenes. Fluorescent tubes produce less heat for a given amount of light, and they have an average life of 6,000 hours, which makes them practical for commercial and museum displays where changing bulbs frequently would be inconvenient or impossible. Perhaps their sole disadvantage is that they require more space than incandescents.

The smallest commonly available fluorescent tubes (usually 4-watt) can be used in most scenes, and they're small enough that two tubes can be used if needed. In fact, I often use two: one light overhead to provide general lighting, and the second for side lighting at the rear of the scene.

Locating the light tubes. Fluorescent tubes can be mounted either on the outer diorama case or the inner

(Top left) Ray's "The Unwelcome Visitors" illustrates the use of brilliant reds and oranges. Note how the painted colors are emphasized by the careful lighting.

(Left) A spectacular back-lit stained glass window in "By Courage I Repel Adversity" shows off yet another striking effect achieved through lighting. The window has one fluorescent tube devoted strictly to it; a second tube provides overall lighting for the box.

(Above) The outer case for "Ettie Belden's $15 Russell" (see page 6), showing the arrangement of the fluorescent tube and its associated components.

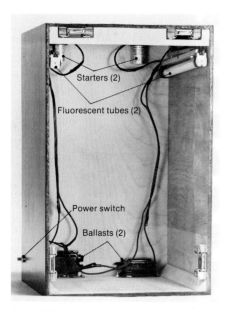

Fig. 1. The interior of the outer case for a typical boxed diorama, showing the lighting components and their locations. This is the case for "The Boy King," shown in color on page 24.

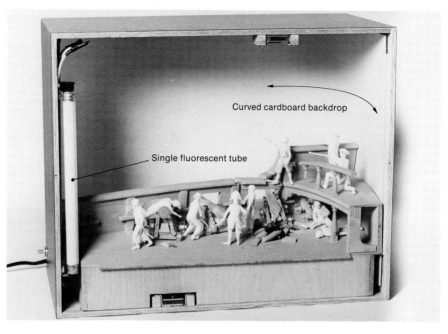

Fig. 2. This in-progress shot of "John Paul Jones" shows a single light tube mounted vertically on the outer case of the diorama. A fallen sail had to be added along the right edge of the scene to keep shadows of the figures from falling on the backdrop.

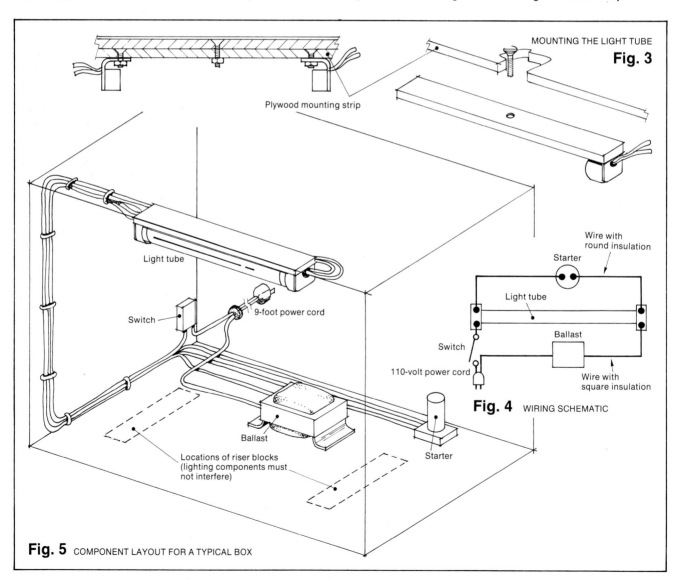

Fig. 5   COMPONENT LAYOUT FOR A TYPICAL BOX

scene. The most common location for the tube that provides general illumination is on the ceiling of the outer case near the front, Fig. 1. Place the light as close as possible to the front edge of the scene so the viewer can't see it. When placing the light at the top front is impossible, the next best location is vertical, along one edge of the scene, Fig. 2. Often, such a mounting can be fastened to the inner scene and hidden behind some feature such as a vertical rock. Tubes used to simulate sunrise or sunset lighting are mounted at the bottom rear of the scene.

A secondary consideration, but important nonetheless, is locating the electrical components where they can be serviced or replaced. In a museum environment where the scenes are on continuously, the tubes will last about three years. Ballast and starter failures are practically nonexistent.

Electrical components. I use three common fluorescent tubes. The 4-watt size is 5¼" long; the 6-watt, 8¼"; and the 8-watt, 11¼". A single 4-watt tube should suffice for a small scene. The components are available packaged in lighting fixtures with a 1" x 1" base, which is convenient for installation but requires more room.

I prefer to separate the individual components of the fixture so the tube will take up a minimum amount of space and the ballast and starter can be mounted in the space behind and underneath the inner scene.

Ballasts come in two shapes, the standard transformer style and a long, narrow shape usually referred to as a "banana" ballast. I prefer the transformer types as they take less space, and some bananas develop an annoying hum. I've also used a combination ballast and starter that requires even less space; these work well.

I prefer to use a starter in the boxes, which preheats the fluorescent tube filaments and is automatically disconnected when the tube fires. (You can eliminate the starter and use a three-wire switch so that you press the switch until the tube fires, then release it.) Whichever arrangement you choose, a full-line lighting store (see your Yellow Pages) should be able to help you find the right components.

Installation and wiring. To allow greater flexibility in mounting the light, I mount the end brackets for the tube on a plywood strip, Fig. 3. I always use 6-32 screws to mount the light fixtures so they can be readily removed. If the tube is to be mounted on the outer case, a 6-32 flathead screw is epoxied in the box before the outer case covering is laminated to the box.

When two or more lights are used, each must have its own starter and ballast. Figure 4 shows a wiring sche-

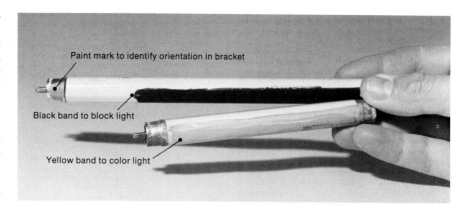

Fig. 6. Two fluorescent tubes from Ray's dioramas. The longer, 6-watt bulb has a stripe of black paint to block light; the 4-watt bulb is tinted with yellow. A. L. Schmidt photo.

Paint mark to identify orientation in bracket

Black band to block light

Yellow band to color light

matic. Standard 110-volt, two-lead lamp wire is used throughout the system. One combined pair will come from each tube end.

The molded insulation on the lamp cord is usually rounded on one conductor and square on the other. I always solder the round insulation wire to the same end-fitting wire at both ends and also to the starter. This may not be necessary, but it makes me feel more comfortable — and I rarely have electrical problems.

I solder all electrical joints, clean them with lacquer thinner, wrap with electrical tape, and secure the tape with a few turns of a heavy thread to prevent the ends from loosening. When the tube is mounted in the top front, I bring both sets of wires down the switch side of the case, mounting the switch at the left rear of the box. I tie the two lines together and run the bundle along the left side and back to the components, Fig. 5. It's important to keep all wires to the minimum length required and to tuck them away where they won't interfere with sliding the scene into the case.

If the light tubes must be mounted on the inner scene, the leads running to

them must be longer so that the scene can be removed from the box. Mount the tubes on the inner assembly and place the unit in front of the outer case, allowing just enough clearance to work inside. Now lace up the light tube leads, run them back to the ballast and starter, and cut to the proper length. Remove the light tube assemblies from the inner scene to make it easier to finish the wiring in the rear of the outer case.

I use a regular 9-foot extension cord for the 110-volt input. Cut off the female plug and feed the end through a small hole drilled in the left rear corner of the outer case. Allow enough lead to attach to the ballast and switch and tie a knot on the inside.

When the wiring is complete, double-check it. Install the light tubes and starter, plug in the power cord, and switch on. The tubes should fire right away; if they don't, try changing the starter (about 10 percent don't work). Leave the system on for several days to see if the ballasts start to hum or growl. This annoying noise is due to the transformer laminations loosening and vibrating; it's not a common problem, but it is better to identify a noisy

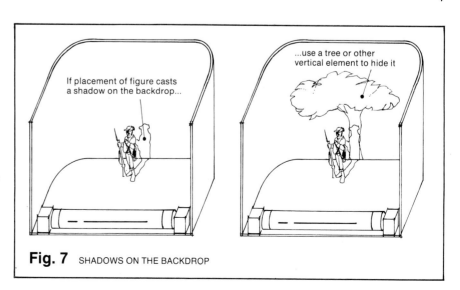

If placement of figure casts a shadow on the backdrop...

...use a tree or other vertical element to hide it

Fig. 7 SHADOWS ON THE BACKDROP

ballast while it's still easy to replace it.

Coloring the light tubes. Inside an enclosed box the light tubes will stabilize at a temperature of roughly 140 degrees F. Acrylic paints will hold up well at this temperature, and their only disadvantage is that the colors are semi-opaque, reducing the transmitted light. I have used colored films, but the acrylics offer more flexibility. For some scenes, just a thin wash adds warmth to the scene. A word of caution: Yellow light may turn your blue sky green!

Several colors can be used on various portions of the tubes, and large sections can be blacked out entirely if required, Fig. 6. I sometimes prepare several tubes, each with a slightly different paint scheme, so I can compare them in the same scene. I place matching spots of color on the tube ferrule and on the adjacent tube fitting to identify the proper tube orientation, because most tubes will have subtle coloring and must be mounted in only one way. Even though the tubes have a life of 6,000 hours, record the final color scheme and paint a spare tube which is taped inside the completed box.

Dealing with shadows. Shadows cast on the background destroy the precious realism that we set out to create. Viewers, seeing a shadow only a fraction of an inch from a figure, quickly realize that the background is not miles away.

It helps to keep the top light as high as possible so that shadows are cast down and behind objects, where viewers can't see them, and to keep figures and other details as far from the backdrop as possible. When this is not possible, position a building edge, tree, or other object precisely at the edge of the shadow, Fig. 7. I've had to add shrubbery in front of a stubborn shadow, or carefully darken the ground next to a shadow to break up a sharp edge, but it's usually possible to disguise a shadow if you're willing to experiment.

Night scenes and special effects. The basic problem in lighting night scenes is that our cardinal rule applies: The light in the box must still overpower the ambient light in the room where it is displayed, because the details must still be visible to the viewer. We can carry off the idea of darkness convincingly by painting the light tube a thin pale blue and using darker colors to paint the scene. A spot or two of orange flame or light (an orange light shining through a cabin window, for example) will make the pale blue appear darker and establish the setting as nighttime.

As soon as we broach the subject of night scenes we begin to tread into the realm of special effects. Just for the fun of it, I once made a boxed diorama depict the passage of 24 hours in 4 minutes. Set outdoors, the scene was of a

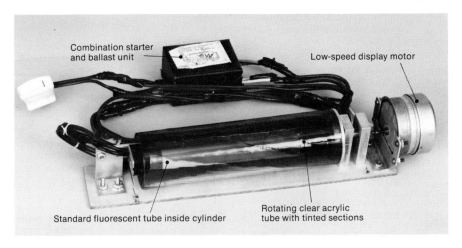

Combination starter and ballast unit

Low-speed display motor

Standard fluorescent tube inside cylinder

Rotating clear acrylic tube with tinted sections

Fig. 8. Ray built this device to cast weirdly changing light patterns beneath the water in "The Swamp," a fantasy diorama (see page 6). The low-speed display motor at right turns the multicolor tinted acrylic cylinder that surrounds the light tube, slowly changing the color and pattern of the light in the scene.

snow-covered, log cabin saloon. Two snow-covered horses were tied up outside. The day-to-night sequence started in daylight; following a red sunset, one by one orange lights appeared in the frosted windows. The sky darkened, then one by one the lights went out and a pale blue full moon lit the scene before a pink sunrise gave way to daylight.

The lighting mechanism consisted of a clear acrylic cylinder around the fluorescent light tube. Portions of the cylinder were tinted with acrylic paints to make the colors cast on the scene change as the cylinder was rotated by a motor. Two cams on the drive shaft controlled the saloon lights, and although it sounds complex, the arrangement was relatively simple (Fig. 8 shows a similar mechanism). I'm sure you can come up with far more complex — and more interesting — possibilities of your own.

Also included under the heading of special effects are small, brightly lit details such as campfires and forges. Figure 9 shows how I've handled such items in a couple of my scenes. Small neon bulbs, which have a life of several thousand hours, make excellent campfires.

That's about it for the lighting lesson. Next time, in the conclusion of this series, we'll look at techniques for modeling convincing water, including the use of plastic compounds. See you then! **FSM**

REFERENCE

● Paine, Sheperd, *How to Build Dioramas*, Kalmbach Publishing Co., Milwaukee, 1980

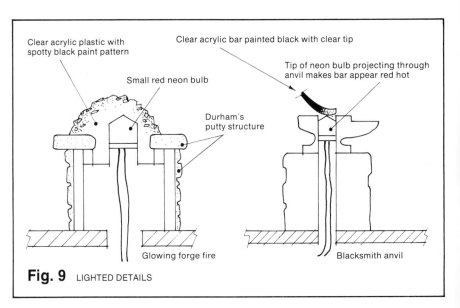

Clear acrylic plastic with spotty black paint pattern

Clear acrylic bar painted black with clear tip

Small red neon bulb

Tip of neon bulb projecting through anvil makes bar appear red hot

Durham's putty structure

Glowing forge fire

Blacksmith anvil

Fig. 9 LIGHTED DETAILS

All photos, Roland Patterson

The high altar of the Benedictine Abbey, Weltenburg, Germany

Ray Anderson's stunning 1/25 scale diorama

RAY ANDERSON of Manhattan Beach, California, told FSM that he wanted to create something extraordinary for his 100th diorama. "My selection was the high altar of the Benedictine Abbey circa 1720 in Weltenburg, Germany, on the Danube," he said. "There wasn't even a close second choice."

While we usually don't publish in-progress photos of models featured in FSM Showcase, we were so impressed by Ray's work that you'll find four such photos of his Benedictine Abbey on page 49.

For this project, Ray said he knew he would use most of the techniques he learned while building previous dioramas. "The natural lighting in the Abbey is dramatic and ideal for a boxed diorama," Ray explained. "I prefer open scenes such as this that can also be enjoyed from a distance. Bringing the details up to the front glass makes the viewer feel a part of the scene. This was accomplished by using the efficient miniature fluorescent lights to overpower the room lighting.

(Top of page) The elaborate outer case of the Weltenburg Abbey diorama is every bit as impressive as the scene inside.

"I prefer to keep the outer case as small as possible, so many of the clearances between the scene and the case are less than ⅛". In designing the outer case, the gray marble molding from the interior was carried around to the exterior. The front face was copied from the main arch separating the high altar from the body of the church. The peaked roof and shingle concept were taken from the building exterior.

"The design was further complicated since I did not want any exposed joints. The design had to be worked out in greater detail than usual, as there was little room for error with the minimum clearances. The inner box assembly is installed from below. Incidentally, I always use metric measurements as they simplify the design and construction. All of the components were scratchbuilt and to the proper scale based on the drawings and photos received from the Abbey."

The base of the diorama is about 12 inches square. The figures are Historex conversions — enlarged to about 60 mm — using the typical shim-and-wedge technique. Ray made the clothing from Kleenex coated with dissolved plastic.

According to Ray, "The dragon and clouds were sculpted

47

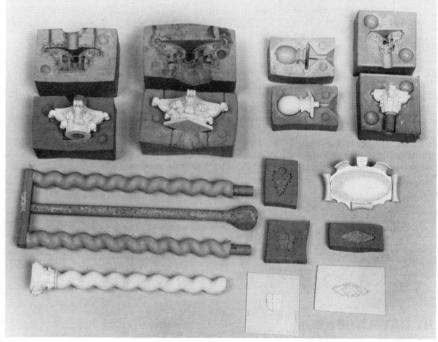

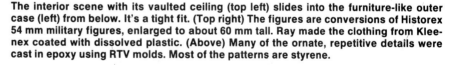

The interior scene with its vaulted ceiling (top left) slides into the furniture-like outer case (left) from below. It's a tight fit. (Top right) The figures are conversions of Historex 54 mm military figures, enlarged to about 60 mm tall. Ray made the clothing from Kleenex coated with dissolved plastic. (Above) Many of the ornate, repetitive details were cast in epoxy using RTV molds. Most of the patterns are styrene.

from A + B epoxy putty. The dragon was coated with dissolved polystyrene so that fine details such as claws and teeth could be made from sheet plastic.

"Many of the details were cast in epoxy using RTV molds. Most of the patterns were made from polystyrene. The rear apse and the ceiling are polyester layups on wooden molds. The shingles are a red flexible polyester on one layer of fine fiberglass cloth." Ray sawed the shingles from the sheets.

The outer case was made from 4.5 mm birch-faced, mahogany-core plywood because it is stable and takes an excellent finish with little effort. "The gray marble molding," Ray said, "was made from basswood for the exterior and the softer jelutong for the interior. The molding was made using a Record multiplane, a modern version of the old Stanley molding plane. It has 36 different blades so practically any molding shape can be duplicated by hand. A precision Inca table saw was used for the jointing. The arched front molding was first cut in narrow circumferential strips using a Hegner jigsaw, then the

individual pieces were cut to the proper shape and glued back together."

Ray explained that he used Humbrol paints "because the colors in boxed dioramas must be dead flat. Rose gold and Testor silver were used. A satin varnish was applied to the simulated marble surfaces. All wood components were primed with gray auto lacquer. The three 4-watt fluorescent tubes were tinted with acrylics."

Ray has been a full-time modeler since 1972; most of his boxed dioramas depict the early American West. He is a Grand Master of the Miniature Figure Collectors of America. **FSM**

Water plays an important role in "The Gossips" — indeed, if it weren't for the skinny-dipping squaw in the shallow pool, there wouldn't be anything to gossip about! Here the squaw figure has been carefully prepared and cast in the tinted polyester resin water.

The art of the diorama

Part 7: Simulating water with plastics

BY RAY ANDERSON

PHOTOS BY ROLAND PATTERSON

THE FROSTING ON THE CAKE, when the cake is a boxed diorama, is realistic water. After all, we've defined a diorama as a scene that tells a story, and almost any kind of water — from an ocean to a mudhole — helps establish the setting for the story. Indeed, water often provides a dramatic element that ranks second only to the figures.

Water is usually the final element I add to a boxed scene, and therein lies a problem. Since the best materials for simulating water are clear liquid plastics, it can be traumatic to pour this messy stuff onto a diorama after all the other painstaking work is complete. In this installment I'll try to pass along tips on materials and techniques to avoid as much of the agony as possible.

The choices. Before we delve into the niceties of using liquid plastic compounds, let's examine the other choices we have for water. Using the real thing is out of the question — it's hard to handle, doesn't look much like water under artificial lighting, and evaporates (and when it doesn't evaporate, things grow in it). Glass, either clear or mirrored, seems like a better bet, but glass is hard to work with, particularly when it comes to shaping it.

Clear acrylic sheet plastic is an excellent choice for settings where we want perfectly still, flat water, Fig. 1. However, sheet plastic is less satisfactory when we want to show water in motion, or want to place figures and objects either submerged in the water or protruding from it. For flowing water that suggests depth, we come right back to liquid, pourable plastics.

The best advice. Since working with liquid plastics can be a smelly and messy business with occasional unpredictable results, you should avail yourself of the best possible help. If you can, locate a firm that formulates a whole family of plastic products (among which will be one for your specific application), and find a genuine technical expert to answer your questions. Perhaps the greatest advantage you gain by dealing with a supplier that formulates the compunds is that you can be sure the products are compatible; for example, you can choose resins, coloring additives, and release agents that you know will work properly together.

In the Los Angeles area we are fortunate to have such a firm, Hastings Plastics (see Sources, below), and the competent staff at Hastings has provided most of the technical advice that I'll present here.

Clear polyester resins similar to the ones I describe are offered by hardware and craft stores. They can be used for simulating water, and many modelers have achieved excellent results with them, but if you have the option, I strongly recommend you deal with a full-service plastics supplier.

"Madame Pumpedoor's Problem" depicts a calamity of sorts: The sheriff has literally hauled the red light district out of town. Here the rain is an important dramatic element in the story, and Ray has managed to suggest it by the glossy top surfaces of the rocks, the convincing mud puddles, and the soaked look of the figures.

Handling and mixing precautions. A few words on handling and mixing polyester resins are in order. You should wear rubber gloves to keep the chemicals off your hands, and work in a well-ventilated area. I use lacquer thinner to clean up the mess, and that requires good ventilation as well.

Use disposable paper cups for mixing, and before you mix, carefully measure water into one cup, mark graduations on it, and keep it as a reference for measuring resin into other cups. And one more handling tip: Carefully clean the threaded tops of the resin containers after each use so you can remove them in the future.

When mixing resin, some air will be trapped. You can let the mixture set as long as possible before pouring, based on the pot life, and when ready to pour, cut a small hole in the bottom of the cup so the solid mixture will flow out and the bubbles will remain behind. Gently heating the mixture to 110° F also helps. I have a small vacuum bell jar that operates off the venturi effect

from a household water faucet, and it pulls a sufficient vacuum to de-air mixed resin.

Hastings recommends an ingenious method of eliminating trapped air. Pour the mixed resin into a Ziploc bag, seal, and knead the mixture to work the air bubbles to the top. When all the air has been collected at the top of the

bag, cut off one bottom corner to drain the resin.

Polyester water pro and con. Because they can be formulated as clear as water and just as thin, polyester resins are the best choice for simulating water — but they have two nasty problems. The first is that polyesters are exothermic, which means they release

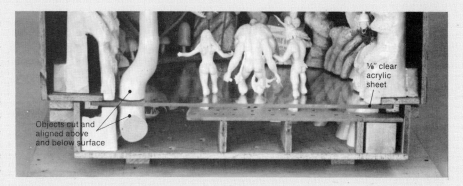

Fig. 1. Clear acrylic sheet was used to simulate water in "The Swamp" (for a color photo of this diorama, see part 1 of this series). Note how all the objects in the water had to be cut apart and aligned above and below the clear plastic.

⅛" clear acrylic sheet

Objects cut and aligned above and below surface

Fig. 2 SETUP FOR POURING WATER

Paper pad added before pouring last resin layer

Thin wood "dam"

Plastic food wrap

Lily pads

Canoe on epoxy support

Prop to hold water base level (angle is exaggerated)

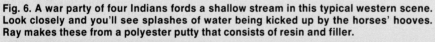

Fig. 4. This quiet scene includes typical multilayer colored polyester resin water. Note the realistic lily pads floating on the water surface, and the big catfish swimming lazily to the right of the canoe, below the paddle.

Fig. 3. This sample shows how styrene details are protected from the harsh polyester resin by a thin coating of clear epoxy. The epoxy, which is hard to see here, extends a fraction of an inch above the water level. FSM photo by A. L. Schmidt.

heat (and expand) while curing; the second is that a polyester surface can remain tacky after curing. We will deal with both problems. On the plus side, polyesters are relatively inexpensive, and the catalyst or hardener is added by volume (with an eyedropper) so polyesters are easy to mix.

The problem of the resin warming and expanding while it cures, then contracting as it cools can be controlled by using a minimum amount of hardener, but that in turn causes other problems. A better method is to pour the resin in several thin layers, allowing the heat to dissipate. Some resins are formulated specifically for shallow pourings, and those are the ones we want.

Polyesters can remain tacky after curing because the hardener, which is much more volatile than the resin, evaporates away from the surface be-

fore doing its job. This leaves the surface layer starved for hardener, and it can stay tacky for a long, long time.

One way to harden the surface layer is to place the diorama scene in a warm place for several days, where the surface will gradually harden on its own. I once used an open metal box containing a 150-watt bulb as a portable oven, which I placed over diorama scenes

Fig. 6. A war party of four Indians fords a shallow stream in this typical western scene. Look closely and you'll see splashes of water being kicked up by the horses' hooves. Ray makes these from a polyester putty that consists of resin and filler.

Fig. 5. Ray stresses making a test pour of resin before applying the material to your diorama. The test ensures compatibility between the resin and the groundwork on the scene. FSM photo by A. L. Schmidt.

while poured polyester water cured.

A second technique is to add a special wax to the resin; the wax will float on the exposed surface, preventing the hardener from evaporating. However, wax may leave a hard-to-remove surface scum. Adding extra hardener will eliminate the tack, but it worsens the heating problems! The solution? Always pour polyester water in several thin layers, and add extra hardener only to the final thin pour, where the heat that it generates is unlikely to cause damage.

Preparing the base. In deep-water scenes, or where the bottom should look like smooth white sand, we can use the plywood scene base as the bottom. It should be smoothly finished and painted white for the sand or medium green for deep water. You'll remember from part 2 that the scene has been constructed with the base rising toward the rear of the box at a 5° angle. The finished water surface will also slope up and away from the front of the box, but at a shallower angle, so the water will be deeper in the foreground, perhaps ⅝" at most, and only ⅛" at the back.

To prepare for the pour, nail a thin wood dam covered with plastic food wrap to the front edge of the scene. Make the top of this dam ¼" higher than the proposed water surface, and use modeling clay to plug gaps where the resin could leak out.

Next, mount floating objects in the scene, suspending them above the plywood. This is tricky, because the waterlines of such objects must coincide with the eventual surface of the water, not the sloping bottom, Fig. 2.

The polyester will attack styrene figures and details, so carefully coat them with clear epoxy to slightly above the water depth, Fig. 3.

Mount details such as lily pads, Fig. 4, on wires, which will fit in holes drilled into the base. A horizontal loop at the top should be at the proposed water level. Glue the painted pads to the stems before pouring the final layer of resin, so the pads remain "floating" on the surface of the water.

Fig. 10. "Thin Ice!" displays the full range of water-making techniques. The froth, splashes, and ice floes are a combination of shaped acrylic and filled-polyester putty.

Pouring resin water. Now we're ready to pour the resin. We'll need a warm, dry, and dust-free area where fumes won't be a problem, because polyester emits a powerful odor. In addition, prepare an aluminum foil cover for the scene to keep out stray dust particles. For the first layer, prop up the front of the scene so the angled bottom is level, Fig. 2.

Use a thin, water-like resin that will flow readily into all the crevices. My choice is Hastings' Hapol 1300-1E, with its MEK Peroxide hardener added at the correct proportion to yield a 90-minute pot life. Limit each pour to ⅛" deep; a greater thickness of resin can generate enough heat and expansion to pull stonework or other detailing away from the base as it cools. (If this should happen, all is not lost: You can save the situation by adding painted swirls of

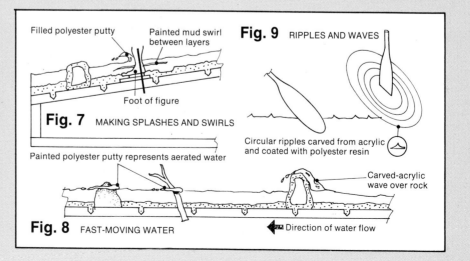

Fig. 7 MAKING SPLASHES AND SWIRLS

Filled polyester putty

Painted mud swirl between layers

Foot of figure

Painted polyester putty represents aerated water

Fig. 8 FAST-MOVING WATER

Fig. 9 RIPPLES AND WAVES

Circular ripples carved from acrylic and coated with polyester resin

Carved-acrylic wave over rock

Direction of water flow

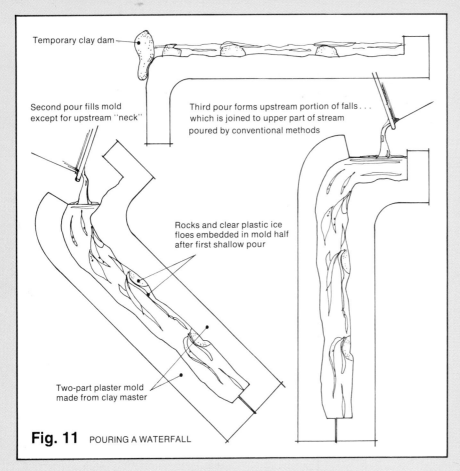

Temporary clay dam

Second pour fills mold
except for upstream "neck"

Third pour forms upstream portion of falls...
which is joined to upper part of stream
poured by conventional methods

Rocks and clear plastic ice
floes embedded in mold half
after first shallow pour

Two-part plaster mold
made from clay master

Fig. 11   POURING A WATERFALL

algae or mud to hide the cracks.)

Adding color. If you like, add a small amount of coloring agent to tint the resin. Use the special colors intended for polyesters; mine come from Hastings, but each product line includes dyes and tints. Blue-green will give depth to deep sea water, and I once added green to represent algae in a Venice canal scene — I've even used a little pearlescent color to add glint and sparkle to water splashes. Keep the color on the light side as there are several more resin layers to come, but remember that the feeling of depth is enhanced when most of the coloring is in the bottom layers. You may want some of the top layers to be clear.

Always make a test pour of resin on a small swatch of groundwork, Fig. 5, to evaluate how the materials will react. This is important, and if you take nothing else away with you from this article, remember this rule: Before pouring polyester on a diorama, TEST it! Among other things, the test will verify that the recommended amount of hardener will indeed cause the resin to cure, and this simple precaution has saved more than one diorama.

Because the resin is very thin, the first layer or two may be absorbed into the porous groundwork. This is to be expected, and merely means you'll have to use one or two more applications to build up the desired depth.

After the first pour cures, double-check that the scene is propped up at the correct angle. A slight adjustment is usually needed, but keep your fingers off the resin while making it! You may want to add fish or other submerged details between pours. Wait until the pour has cured, then epoxy the item into place and use epoxy to fill undercuts where air might be trapped.

Pour the second 1/8" layer and continue to fine tune the tilt of the scene and the coloring until the full depth of the water is achieved. The final pour should be about 1/16" deep, and I use twice the recommended amount of hardener, in my case, 12 drops of hardener per ounce instead of 6. This will provide sufficient catalyst to cure the surface in spite of evaporation.

Now let the completed water sit undisturbed for several days while you recover.

Shallow water. Next let's take a look at three different water applications. For a shallow, meandering creek, Fig. 6, the water base should slope up at a 5° angle toward the rear of the scene. The water should be about 1/4" deep in front and taper to 1/8" at the back. Figures in the stream should be mounted before the groundwork is added, and rocks or fallen branches are nice additions. Footprints can be pressed into the creek bed when the groundwork is applied.

After establishing the water level as

has been described, pour in about 1/8" of resin at the front. It will soak into the groundwork, but do not add more — doing so can cause a surface skin to form. If the skin forms and the liquid beneath it soaks into the groundwork, the result will be unsightly voids.

I added swirls of tan paint around the horses' hooves in the stream and coming out of the hoofprints in the creek bed, Fig. 7. These should be added when there is about 1/16" of cured resin over the ground. When the final layer has cured, add surface splashes from the hooves with translucent polyester putty using a toothpick. I make my own polyester putty by adding Hastings' Cab-O-Sil 151 to the resin until I have the required stiffness.

Fast-moving water. Faster-running streams will probably be in a rock structure with some rocks protruding from the stream. Basically the same procedure will be followed, except that there will be streaks of aerated water flowing around and over the rocks, Fig. 8. These are made from the polyester putty, with pearlescent color and white paint added between the layers of resin. The surface splashes will extend out of the resin.

I have not found a simple way to create large waves breaking over a rock, bow waves, or the circular waves radiating from a canoe paddle in smooth water. The technique I use is cumbersome, but the results are realistic. I shape the waves with a flat bottom out of chunks of clear acrylic sheet using rotary tools, and smooth them with rubber abrasive wheels, Fig. 9. They are cemented in place on the cured resin surface with dabs of polyester, then a thin coat of resin is brushed over the ripples. All the joints and fine tool marks disappear, leaving a realistic water surface.

Why not manipulate the resin while it cures to work in ripples and waves? I know it's possible, because I've read of modelers doing it, but I've always been reluctant to tamper with the resin while it sets. I far prefer the conservative approach of making waves the hard way, but being in control of the precise contours I achieve, Fig. 10.

Modeling a waterfall. The waterfall in "A Problem on the Powder River" (Part 1) was an attempt to see how far I could carry the basic process of simulating water. When all the stonework was in place and painted, a full-size clay model of the falling water was made; both front and back were sculptured. The clay piece consisted of the vertical water column and about 1" of the right-angle bend upstream.

The next step was to make a two-piece (front and back) plaster mold, Fig. 11. To cast the mold, the rear section was positioned horizontally and a clay dam added at the start of the transition at the top. A coat of resin was poured in and allowed to cure, then protruding rocks and frothy foam were added. More resin and foam were added in ⅛" steps until the mold was nearly filled. The two halves were then taped together and filled with resin up to the start of the 90° transition. Before taking the mold apart, it was repositioned once more to cast the transition.

When the final pour had cured, the mold was removed. Additional spray was added to the front of the falls, and the completed casting epoxied to the scene. The upstream water was poured in steps onto the gravel bed and blended into the falls with a rubber wheel in a motor tool. Then the lower edge was puttied to a turbulent, ice-choked pool. The rear of this pool tumbled into a deep canyon. The results were realistic with the foam and submerged rocks in the transparent water.

And if all else fails. I don't want to leave you with the impression that I have all the answers, because polyester is tricky stuff to use. Years ago, while researching an Indian diorama, I found reference to an obscure dance dealing with "bad water." I immediately knew they were talking about polyester. At dawn, on the days that I will be pouring, I go up on the roof and, facing east, do the dance. It seems to work as well as anything.

This installment concludes our series on building dioramas. I hope my ideas and techniques will serve as a jumping-off point for your own dioramas, and that in years to come I'll have a chance to look at the results you've achieved here in the pages of FSM. Oh yes, before I go, one final word of advice: Always — that's ALWAYS — make sure that each diorama you set out to build has a story to tell! **FSM**

REFERENCE

● Williamson, Bob, editor, *The Breakthrough Habitat and Exhibit Manual*, Breakthrough Publications, Loganville, Georgia, 1986

SOURCES

● Castolite, P. O. Box 391, Woodstock, IL 60098
● Hastings Plastics Company, 1704 Colorado Avenue, Santa Monica, CA 90404
● Sculpture Associates Ltd., 40 East 19th Street, New York, NY 10003
● Wildlife Artist Supply Company, P. O. Box 967, Monroe, GA 30655

Afterword and acknowledgments

In a comparatively short time the boxed diorama has evolved from a curiosity into an accepted form of modeling, and as the genre has matured, much of its potential has been realized. Although there's lots of territory left to explore, with the medium relatively mature, I think I can say a few things about what may and may not work in the future.

With the new home computers, it is now possible to store sound on a solid-state circuit chip, providing a sound unit sufficiently rugged and compact to be part of the box. Crude tests indicate that sound is a legitimate dimension to add to boxed scenes.

On the other hand, attempts at animating boxed dioramas have largely been unsuccessful; the results I've seen suggest that movement is best left to some other medium. To my mind, a boxed scene best tells its story by freezing or suggesting movement, not by replicating it.

I owe a special thanks to Gene Favell, founder of the Favell Museum, for his support, encouragement, and friendship. Special thanks, many times over, are also due to "Pat" Patterson, whose excellent photographs made the magazine series possible. He has photographed over 100 of my diorama scenes, and I recall only one shot that was unusable. Thanks also to my good friend and severest critic, Clive Von Wooster. He has the uncanny ability to find the most minute anatomical imperfection in my figures — and has never hesitated to tell me about it.

Last, but not least, a word of thanks to *FineScale Modeler* Magazine. I was delighted when FSM Editor Bob Hayden suggested reprinting my articles in book form, and I sincerely hope that the convenience of having all the material in one place will encourage more modelers to experiment with the boxed diorama medium.

Dedication

This book is dedicated to all my fellow box builders who have had to develop the many diversified skills required on their own — the hard way. Like me, most have spent countless lonely hours at their workbench, agonizing over a problem and wondering whether there might be someone to help. In the early days of boxed dioramas kindred souls were few and far between, and even protracted pondering over a problem eventually yielded the same old conclusion: "Solve it yourself!"

Ray Anderson
March 1988

Index